D1121231

AMERICAN BERSERK

A Cub Reporter,

a Small-Town Daily,

the Schizo '70s

BILL MORRIS

SUNBURY
P R E S S
Mechanicsburg, PA USA

Published by Sunbury Press, Inc.
Mechanicsburg, Pennsylvania

SUNBURY
P R E S S

www.sunburypress.com

For information about special discounts for bulk purchases, please contact Sunbury Press Orders Dept. at (855) 338-8359 or orders@ sunburypress.com.

To request one of our authors for speaking engagements or book signings, please contact Sunbury Press Publicity Dept. at publicity@ sunburypress.com.

ISBN: 978-1-62006-823-6 (Trade paperback)
ISBN: 978-1-62006-808-3 (Mobipocket)

Library of Congress Control Number: 2016963024

FIRST SUNBURY PRESS EDITION: March 2017

Product of the United States of America
0 1 1 2 3 5 8 13 21 34 55

Set in Bookman Old Style
Designed by Crystal Devine
Cover by Lawrence Knorr
Edited by Janice Rhayem

Continue the Enlightenment!

To the memory of my mother,
Anne Slusher Morris (1920-1977)

Author's Note

This is a work of nonfiction. Care has been taken to check facts and to identify surmise and speculation as such. Quoted speech is taken from one or more of the following sources: author interviews, published accounts, my personal memories, trial transcripts, an unpublished nonfiction manuscript, and recollections of one or more persons who were present when the quoted conversation took place. Since one of this book's themes is the slippery nature of memory, I can't guarantee iron-clad accuracy. The gifted memoirist Mary Karr spoke to this slipperiness when she claimed to remember the smell of Juicy Fruit gum on a boy she kissed in junior high, nearly forty years ago: "Maybe the boy I kissed was chewing Bazooka Joe or Dubble Bubble, say. But I think in this case the specific memory—even if wrong—is permissible, because readers understand the flaws of memory and allow for them." I hope she's right. Any errors of fact in this book are entirely the fault of its author.

"Memories are creative. To treat memory as a fact is nonsense. It's inescapably fiction." – *Aleksandar Hemon*

"(M)emory consists of constructing, and later reconstructing, narratives, not just storing and retrieving data. Memory is an imaginative act; first we imagine what we'll want to keep and then we fashion stories from what we've kept. Memories don't just happen, they are built." – *Walter Kirn*

"Writing is recalling." – *Karl Ove Knausgaard*

Contents

PART ONE

In a Strange Land

The Summons

The summons came while I was away from home, off working my shit job at the Record Bar in Friendly Shopping Center. This was Greensboro, North Carolina, in the bicentennial autumn of 1976. The only good thing about my job at the Record Bar was the daily task of vacuuming the store's hectare of burnt-orange shag carpeting because the roar of the Hoover upright drowned out the dreck coming over the store's sound system—the current hits by Fleetwood Mac, Elton John and Kiki Dee, the Captain and Tenille, and the one that never failed to make me want to reach for the revolver, Peter Frampton's "Show Me the Way," with that cheesy talking guitar.

It was the '70s, it was the Age of Cheese. A time when America had sunk into a stylistic Sargasso featuring such flotsam as disco, soft rock, platform shoes, wide lapels and wider neckties, leisure suits, shag haircuts and shag carpeting, water beds, pet rocks, talking guitars, and cars that were shoddy, ugly, and sometimes dangerous, with names like Gremlin, Cordoba, and Ford's highly flammable Pinto. Even baseball, that most timeless of games, had succumbed to the era's cheese: men in Fu Manchu moustaches and Technicolor polyester playing in ashtray-shaped stadiums on fields made of synthetic AstroTurf. Politics were super-cheesy, with a peanut-farming Baptist from Georgia running for president against a dim-bulb incumbent who got the job only because the vice president and president who came before him were a couple of stone crooks.

When I got home from the Record Bar that night, my sister Gretchen told me about the summons—a phone call from a man named Bob Collins in Chambersburg, Pennsylvania, with an outfit called *Public Opinion*. I had never heard of the man or the town, and I assumed *Public Opinion* was some kind of polling service, like Gallup. Why would a polling service call me? I'd spent the five months since my college graduation pinballing up and down the Eastern Seaboard, from upstate New York to low-country Georgia, knocking on doors at newspapers and begging editors to hire me as a reporter. *Come back when you've got some more clips to show us,* they always said. After hearing that a couple dozen times I had to swallow the urge to shout back, *How the hell am I supposed to get more clips if you won't give me a fucking job?*

But I never shouted back, because, truth to tell, I was supremely unqualified for a reporter's job. In college, I'd taken a single creative writing course and no journalism classes for the simple reason that the school didn't offer any. All I had to show at those job interviews was a handful of clips from my school newspaper—sketches, really—and a couple of articles from a free weekly, including a long interview with the brash new mayor of Providence, Rhode Island, a felon-in-training named Buddy Cianci. Instead of readying myself for the job market while in college, I'd become absorbed with researching and writing a book-length history of Providence, a city that fascinated me then and fascinates me still. All I knew for sure when I graduated was that I wanted to become a writer—a real writer, a novelist—and like many who'd come before me, I believed that the whirlwind of a daily newspaper's city room would be an ideal place to serve my apprenticeship.

To make matters worse, it was a buyer's job market. America may have been sinking into a stylistic Sargasso, but American journalism was entering a golden age. Gifted practitioners of New Journalism—Grover Lewis, Gay Talese, Joan Didion, Tom Wolfe, and many others— were using the novelist's tools to fashion astonishing long-form nonfiction. Daily newspapers were also producing superb work, and basking in fat profits. Woodward and Bernstein had just helped send the president and a boatload of his minions into early retirement, and it suddenly seemed that every last one of my brightest contemporaries wanted to be a newspaper reporter. Hard to believe today, but journalism was seen as a glamorous, even noble calling. My timing was atrocious.

So I wasn't feeling particularly optimistic the next day when I returned Bob Collins's phone call. It turned out that *Public Opinion* was a 20,000-circulation, Gannett-owned daily newspaper in Chambersburg, Pennsylvania, the seat of Franklin County, a dozen miles north of the Mason-Dixon Line and roughly midway between Pittsburgh and Philadelphia. Collins was the president and publisher, and he said he'd heard good things about me from a fellow Gannett editor who had interviewed me and told me to come back when I had more clips, blah, blah, blah. Collins wanted to know when I would be able to come up for a job interview. Not if, when.

That was when I did one of the more immaculately bone-headed things in a long history of doing bone-headed things: I demurred. I told Collins I needed to think it over, because I was having car trouble, and it would be tough for me to travel 350 miles each way. My car was a 1954 Buick Century, I explained, more clunker than classic, and I didn't have enough money at the moment to get it fixed. I'm sure Collins was aghast that I wasn't jumping at the chance to come up for a job interview. I was working as a clerk at a Record Bar, for chrissakes.

That evening, my sister had been invited to a cookout, and she took me along. Gretchen was entering her last year as a dance major at the University of North Carolina's Greensboro campus, and I'd offered to drive her down to school from our parents' home in Syracuse, New York, after my fruitless summer of post-graduation job hunting. I still have a snapshot of that drive with Gretchen and my dog Amos. I can remember the blast furnace late-summer heat as we approached the North Carolina state line, windows rolled down, Amos in the back seat with his nose stuck into the on-rush of hot air. When "A Fifth of Beethoven" by Walter Murphy & the Big Apple Band came over the Buick's Sonomatic AM radio, Gretchen and I were so delirious we cranked up the volume and pounded on the car's roof to the ridiculous song's beat, grateful for anything that took our minds off the hell we were passing through. When we got to Greensboro, Gretchen helped me get a job washing dishes at a deli-jazz club called Sammy's, where she was waiting tables. Before long I got the job at the Record Bar, which, come to think of it, was actually a step up. Gretchen said I could sleep on her sofa, rent-free, until I got my life sorted out.

That night's cookout was hosted by one of Gretch-
en's favorite teachers, Gay Cheney, a tall woman with
salt-and-pepper curls and a coiled intensity. Over beers
in the back yard, Gay asked me what I was up to. I
explained that I was going to be a writer, then I told
her about that day's invitation to a job interview in
Pennsylvania.

"So when's the interview?" she asked. There it was
again—not if, when.

"I don't think I'm going," I said. "I've been going to
job interviews for months, and it's always the same shit:
come back when you have some more clips to show us. I'm
over it. The only way to become a novelist is to sit down
and write a novel." I believed that then, and I believe it
now. I had already written and discarded an apprentice
novel, and I'd recently made several weekend trips from
Greensboro to my parental hometowns of Athens, Georgia, and Bluefield, West Virginia, with the vague notion
of writing a multi-generational novel about a Southern
family. Hardly the most original of ideas.

Gay's face darkened. I could see that she was actually angry. "You're discouraged because you've spent a
few *months* going to interviews, and you haven't gotten
a job yet? You've got no right to be discouraged. If you
let a little rejection like this stop you, you'll never make
it as a writer or any other kind of artist. *Never.*"

Her words hit me like a punch. I started to protest,
but I stopped, because I knew she was right.

The next day I learned that a buddy who owned a
'57 Chevy, more classic than clunker, was heading to
New Jersey to visit his family, and he offered to drop me
off in Chambersburg on his way up I-81. I would hitch-
hike back from the job interview. I called Bob Collins
and told him I was on my way. A stranger named Gay
Cheney had changed the course of my life.

The Offer

On a raw October afternoon I climbed out of my buddy's '57 Chevy and stood looking across Chambersburg's North Third Street at the offices of *Public Opinion*. The building, as I would soon learn, had been a passenger station on the Cumberland Valley Railroad when it was built after the Civil War. Its walls were now a pleasing pale yellow, and its tall windows were blocked by venetian blinds. I pictured people doing serious and important work behind those blinds.

Bob Collins turned out to be a sandy-haired terrier from New Jersey with rolled-up shirtsleeves and a staccato way of talking that said *newspaperman*. His eyes drilled me through thick-rimmed glasses. He looked like he hadn't started shaving yet, but he also looked like he could smell bullshit when he was a mile upwind from it. I liked him instantly and wanted him to like me, maybe because I sensed that this was to be my last chance, and I had come to understand, way deep in my bones, that I did not want to go back to the Record Bar and Peter Frampton's talking guitar.

Collins smoked one Merit cigarette after another as he peppered me with questions through the late afternoon. He seemed impressed that I'd earned a degree from an Ivy League university, maybe because he hadn't finished college. I didn't see the sense of informing him that it had taken me six years to get that degree, or that I'd scraped by with the absolute minimum number of credits. The reason it took me six years was because after my sophomore year I decided college was a waste of time, and if I wanted to be a novelist I needed to leave the shaded grove and go out into the world to gather that precious substance known as experience, the stuff novels are made of. So I took an indefinite "leave of absence"—no sense burning bridges even though I had no intention of returning to school—and got a job as a farmhand at a spread in southwestern Vermont that boarded broken-down thoroughbred racehorses from nearby Green Mountain Park. This was the last stop for many of these nags before they were turned into dog chow or glue.

I was terrified of the huge, jittery horses, but I found I loved the manual labor, baling hay, digging post holes, cleaning stalls, putting a roof on a barn, and I was thrilled to be accepted as the long-haired oddball on a raffish blue-collar crew that consisted of a ham-faced Vermont farmer, a hard-drinking cowboy with a broken leg, a petty-criminal greaser who had his eye on the foreman's hottie sixteen-year-old daughter, and a gifted old black trainer who nowadays would be called a horse whisperer. That summer was when I acquired Amos, a black-and-white springer spaniel pup with a brown left eye and an arresting blue right eye. We became inseparable.

When the racing season ended, I pocketed my $500 life savings and drove Amos cross-country in the Buick's predecessor, a wheezing '54 Chevy pickup, top speed 40 m.p.h. It took us a week to get from Texarkana to El Paso, Texas. I then worked a string of odd jobs up and down the coast of California, in kitchens and vineyards, dairy farms and orchards. At night I worked on my apprentice novel, a murder story set on a Vermont racehorse farm, but the main thing I learned was how far I had to go before I would be able to consider myself a beginner. After a couple of years of this, I asked myself if I wanted to spend the rest of my life working minimum-wage jobs to support my writing. In my roundabout way I was coming to understand that experience is not all it's cracked up to be. As Flannery O'Connor, one of my favorite writers, put it, "The fact is that anybody who has survived his childhood has enough information about life to last him the rest of his days. If you can't make something out of a little experience, you probably won't be able to make it out of a lot. The writer's business is to contemplate experience, not be merged in it."

If I wanted to become a novelist, in other words, I didn't need to wander the world harvesting experiences. I needed to figure out a way to get paid to contemplate experience and then write about it. The best way to do that, I reasoned, would be to do as my father had done and get a job as a newspaper reporter. But this was the season of Watergate, and I knew it would be impossible to land a coveted reporter's job without a college degree. So I sold my pickup in Sebastopol, California, and Amos and I boarded a hippie bus in San Francisco's Haight-Ashbury, a retrofitted 1950s GMC Coach with mattresses instead of seats, the air thick with marijuana smoke and patchouli. We headed east. The backup driver had failed to show up, and when we made it to Wyoming in the small hours of the following morning, the weary driver turned to me and asked if I could drive the bus. I lied and said I could. So I got behind the wheel and pushed the bus and its forty-two human passengers and two dogs into the Wyoming night, feeling like Neal Cassady. I wound up driving about half of the rest of the trip with the help of nothing stronger than coffee, diet pills, and the inexplicable energy of youth—until the

Pennsylvania Turnpike, when my fried eyeballs started seeing gigantic frogs hopping across the highway and I suggested it might be a good idea to let the real driver take the wheel. That fall, after a two-year absence, I returned to the shaded grove, where Amos accompanied me to all my classes, snoozing quietly under my chair.

I decided not to mention any of this personal history to Bob Collins, or the fact that the novelist who'd taught my one creative writing course, a randy old goat named R. V. Cassill, had needed all of six words to assess my prospects as a writer of fiction: "Works hard but possesses limited talent." *Up yours!*, I remember thinking at the time. Instead of dwelling on these facts or my meager collection of clips, I tried to steer the conversation around to that history of Providence I'd written during my junior and senior years. Surely, I suggested, anyone who has the discipline to research and write a history book can learn how to write newspaper articles.

Collins, miraculously, bought it. He offered me a job covering several area school boards and the local women's college, adding I would be free to write as many "enterprise" stories on the side as I wanted. I loved the sound of that word *enterprise*. It was so open-ended, so make-it-up-as-you-go-along, like something that might blossom into the writing of fiction.

Now Collins asked me how much money I would need to start, the worst question a job applicant can face, even worse than "What do you see yourself doing five years from now?"

I picked a number out of the air. "How about a hundred and fifty a week?"

"How about a hundred and forty?" Collins countered. It was better than minimum wage, though not by much. I took it.

Gannett had a strict policy forbidding overtime pay, Collins went on, so if I worked more than forty hours a week I was to keep track of the hours and then take time off with pay. Already I was learning the key ingredients in Gannett's recipe for success: buy the newspaper in a one-paper town, hire fresh meat straight out of college, control payroll with an iron fist, then jack up ad rates for every schmuck haberdasher, restaurateur, and car dealer in your circulation area. They'll squawk, but they'll be forced to pay up. And you'll get rich.

Collins and I still had one thing to iron out: When could I start? The presidential election was just a couple of weeks away, and Collins seemed to assume I would be eager to be a part of the staff's election night coverage. But I needed to hitch-hike back to North Carolina, fix the Buick, then drive up to my parents' house in Syracuse to fetch some clothes and books and cooking utensils. I suggested I report for work on November 8, the Monday *after* Election Day.

Collins gave me a quizzical look. Without realizing it, I had just set the tone for everything that was to come. What I was saying was that I wanted to skip election night precisely because it was a major news event that came along every four years, the sort of prefab story that requires no enterprise on the part of a reporter. I had no desire to be a member of a pack covering a "big" story that was, essentially, canned.

Where did this impulse come from? Most likely it came out of the footlocker in the cobwebby attic of the house where I grew up in suburban Detroit. One endless summer afternoon, when I was about eight or nine years old, I was trying to kill my boredom by poking around the attic, where I discovered a few treasures amid the junk, including my father's jodhpurs and lace-up riding boots from his time with the US Army's First Cavalry in the Pacific. I remember being amazed: *My father rode horses in a war that was ended by atom bombs.* When I came to the battered footlocker, I opened it slowly, hoping for something nice and creepy, maybe a bloody bayonet or a Japanese skull.

Instead I found black-and-white photographs and piles of yellowing newspapers. A much younger version of my father was in most of the pictures, and the newspapers were old editions of *The Washington Post*, published before I was born. I noticed that every one of them had at least one story that appeared under the words *By Richard Morris, Post Staff Writer*.

When I asked my father about this, he explained that those things were called by-lines and, yes, he had written all of those stories. Now I was doubly amazed: It was possible to write stories and have them printed under your name in a newspaper that was read every day by thousands of strangers. Even at that young age, I sensed that this was something worth wanting. I asked my father how it felt.

"Let me tell you a little something," he said in the honeyed Georgia drawl he never lost, even after spending most of his adult life in the frosty far North. "Seeing something you've written in print is like having your back scratched. But seeing something you've written in print with your name on it, well now, that's like having your back scratched by Marilyn Monroe."

I couldn't imagine why anyone would want to have a movie star scratch his back, but I never forgot the awe I heard in my father's voice that day.

One of the photographs in that footlocker was taken in the *Post* newsroom on an election night. I've always wanted to believe it was 1948, the night of DEWEY DEFEATS TRUMAN, and this is possible because my father had left *The Richmond Times-Dispatch* to join the *Post* in the summer of '48. But I'll never be sure of the date, because my father died in 2008, before I thought to ask him when that picture was taken.

My father is on the right side of the frame pouring from a big hobo coffee pot for a fellow reporter named Ray Pittman, who is holding his saucer in both hands, beaming. Other men—and it was only men in that news-room—are bellying up to a large table that's littered with the familiar newsroom clutter: old papers, a phone book, a copy spike. But in the center of the table is a hint that this is a special night: a large, oval tray loaded with cups and saucers, carefully wrapped sandwiches, sugar bowls and glass bottles of milk. There is a map of the world on the wall. You can almost hear the ringing of telephones, the clacking of typewriters, the mutter of a police radio. The picture is, above all, a portrait of a man's world. The only feminine touch is provided by my father, whose left pinkie is extended, almost primly, to keep the lid from falling off the coffee pot. These men belonged to a tribe, and every last one of them was glowing with gratitude that a major news story had made its scheduled appear-ance and for one night at least, tonight, election night, there would be free coffee and sandwiches and no one would have to think for himself. Tonight the news was being served up on a tray. It wasn't the cozy bonhomie of that all-male tribe that put me off. It was the gratitude on the men's faces.

With obvious reluctance, Collins agreed to let me report for work the Monday after the election. Then he led the way from his office and out through the deserted advertising department, a room with a buffed linoleum floor, orange walls, tidy desks with flowers and family pictures, the place where the money was made. When we entered the cave of the newsroom, my heart actually started to race. This was the world hidden behind the venetian blinds. This was where my life as a professional writer would begin.

The ceiling was black, and the yellowish brick walls reminded me that I needed to get my teeth cleaned. The frayed carpet was the color of a sidewalk. The light came from cold, white fluorescent tubes suspended from the ceiling. Piles of newspapers teetered on most desks alongside ashtrays with rounded mounds of butts. Every reporter's desk had its own telephone and its own red IBM Selectric typewriter, while the editors' desks had those new-fangled computers with screens that looked like miniature television sets. There were only a few people in the room, reading newspapers, murmuring into telephones. The one exotic touch was the row of clocks along one wall, each one set to the wrong local time in some faraway world capital—Moscow, London, Paris. Low-rent Walter Cronkite, I thought.

That was when the smell hit me—a bosky perfume made of newsprint, dust, grease, and ink. The smell was emanating from the pressroom, which was next to the newsroom, a cavern with an ancient Goss letterpress that was silent at this hour, having long ago completed its thundering noontime run. That Goss press looked like some primordial beast that had just crawled out of a tar pit. It wasn't until years later that I learned *Public Opinion* had been one of a half-dozen papers that offered use of its press to print scab copies of *The Washington Post* during a bitter pressmen's strike in DC in the fall of 1975. That gesture said everything you needed to know about Gannett's attitude toward labor unions.

The smell in that pressroom transported me to the days of my boyhood paper route, the after-school ritual of folding a couple dozen copies of *The Pontiac Press*, packing them into the canvas bag knotted to my Schwinn's handlebars, then firing them onto customers' porches as I whizzed along the sidewalk. The ink turned my fingers black, and the newsprint gave off the same pulpy perfume I was smelling now. Only now, instead of delivering newspapers, I would be helping to create them.

Just then a man came through a back door that led to a loading dock. He brought a gust of chill air with him and the scent of a recent cigarette. Collins introduced me to Brad Bumsted, the paper's "star reporter," who covered the Franklin County commissioners, major trials, spectacular crimes, anything that would land his improbable by-line on the front page. Bumsted was short like Collins but built like a beer keg. With his mud-brown hair and cheap sport coat, he looked more like a cop than a newspaper reporter. As he shook my hand, he took his time sizing up the new competition.

Getting hired must have made me feel cocky, because I blurted out, "You like your job, Brad?"

"Yeah, I do," he said. "Very much."

"You like covering the commissioners and courts?"

"I said yeah. I do."

"I wouldn't mind having that beat myself."

I immediately thought, *What an asshole!* My pushiness was totally out of character. Brad moved past me into the newsroom without another word, but I noticed Collins was smiling. He liked his reporters brash and pushy, and he told me years later that he knew right then he'd been smart to offer me a job.

IT WAS LATE AFTERNOON when I left the building, as high as I've ever been in my life. Though dusk was coming and I had a lot of hitchhiking ahead of me, I decided to take a walk to the middle of town, just a few blocks away. On the way I paused in front of an old frame house to read a historical marker that said the abolitionist John Brown had boarded there in the summer of 1859 while in Chambersburg to pick up guns and ammunition for his looming raid on the federal arsenal at Harpers Ferry, West Virginia. According to the plaque, Brown, the clever dog, used the name "Smith" as an alias. The building was more shack than shrine. It looked forlorn, its two ground-floor windows and cellar window boarded up, its gutters sagging, no railings on the front steps, the clapboards and upstairs shutters in need of paint. Even the sidewalk and curbstones were cracked. It was obvious the residents of Chambersburg didn't much care about local history. Or maybe Gettysburg, just twenty-five miles to the east, had stolen all the thunder.

In the town square the handsome Franklin County Courthouse gazed down on a grassy island adorned with a fountain and a Union soldier who was facing south, keeping an eternal vigil in case the Rebels decided to come back for more. This was no ordinary country crossroads. This was the intersection of US 30, the Lincoln Highway, and US 11, the Molly Pitcher Highway. US 30 was America's first transcontinental road, linking the Oregon coast to the New Jersey shore, and US 11 runs from the Canadian border to the Gulf of Mexico. These were local paths of commerce and war for Indians

of the Six Nations long before a Scots-Irish immigrant named Benjamin Chambers arrived in 1730 and, with the blessing of the Penn family, built mills at the confluence of Conococheague Creek and Falling Spring, a few hundred yards from where I was standing. I could see the Appalachian Mountains rising bluely to the west.

Other than the passing cars and trucks and the plastic cladding on several storefronts, the downtown looked much as it had in the nineteenth century, when, according to two more historical plaques, Chambersburg was a major way station on the Underground

Railroad as well as a repeat target of Confederate vengeance. J. E. B. Stuart came in 1862 to burn railroad buildings and steal guns, horses, and eight Negroes. In late June of 1863, Robert E. Lee led the Army of Northern Virginia through town on its way to the gathering storm at Gettysburg. The following summer, with the war turning into a lost cause, Confederate Brigadier General John McCausland demanded $500,000 from the townsfolk as reparation for the Yankee burning and looting of the Shenandoah Valley. When the Chambersburg town fathers told him they couldn't possibly come up with the money, McCausland, following the orders of Lieutenant General Jubal Early, told his troops to torch the place. The soldiers, many of them drunk on looted liquor, happily complied. More than four hundred buildings burned, including the Franklin County Courthouse, which was reduced to a charred brick shell and later rebuilt. This meant the downtown I was seeing was mostly post-Civil War buildings.

Walking the two miles back to the interstate, I was delighted by the town's ghostly history and its nineteenth-century feel, the Mansard roofs, the broad porches on solid brick and stone houses, the many humble frame houses like the one where John Brown paused on the way to his doom.

Passing those houses, some elegantly maintained, others downright shabby, I could glimpse people inside fixing dinner, watching TV, reading the newspaper. In a few days they would be reading words I had written. Though I found this thrilling, I also felt a stab of anxiety about coming to this small town—this backwater—to live and work. Would any interesting stories unfold? Would I be bored? Lonely? Would writing for a newspaper really prepare me for writing novels?

Events—brutal, bloody, freakish events—would provide a blunt answer to my questions soon enough. A more elegant answer was put forth by the journalist Marshall Frady in a *Life* magazine article about the novelist Jesse Hill Ford and his peculiar triumphs and travails in the small town of Humboldt, Tennessee. Frady could have been thinking about me in Chambersburg, or any writer in any small town anywhere in the world, when he wrote these words:

> Such small towns are particularly felicitous locations in which to set up in the business of writing novels. They really contain, in microcosm, the whole of mankind's career: all the history of the human heart is replayed within the passage of one small-town generation. One can perceive the full course of lives, the rise and fall of ambitions, the strugglings and spoilings of lust – one sees and knows the beginnings and the ends. Curiously, it is in a small community that a writer's sense of the mortal experience on this planet can most nearly assume universal perspectives.

As I was about to learn, Frady got it exactly right.

Baptism

My memory told me that after reporting for work on Monday, November 8, as Collins and I had agreed, I spent my first days on the job getting pointers from various editors, calling school sources to introduce myself, and getting acquainted with my fellow reporters, who were young, driven, and generally welcoming.

The microfilm of that Monday afternoon's paper tells a different story: I got my first by-line on my very first day on the job. It was a double by-line with Brad Bumsted above a front-page story about a fugitive in a local murder case who'd been arrested out of state by the FBI. Re-reading the article so many years later, I could vaguely recall making phone calls as the noon deadline bore down, then watching over Brad's shoulder as he wrote the story, amazed that anyone could type so fast using just his thumbs and index fingers. He not only looked like a cop, he typed like a cop. A vanished memory was being replaced by a milky one I didn't entirely trust. I seemed to be constructing a memory to fit newly unearthed facts.

Our story carried a Garden City, New York, dateline even though Brad and I had not left the newsroom to do the reporting—a routine if misleading sleight of hand designed to give readers the impression that *Public Opinion*'s dogged reporters would travel hundreds of miles to get a story. The truth was, despite those wall clocks pegged to the local time in faraway capitals, we rarely traveled more than twenty-five miles to report a story. Brad had another front-page by-line that day on a story about another local crime suspect picked up by police out of state. That one carried a Winchester, Virginia, dateline. Brad Bumsted really got around.

So the first thing I learned was that my very earliest memories were flawed. There had been no settling-in period. It was sink or swim from day one. I should have expected no less from Gannett.

My second by-line appeared the next day under this heart-stopping headline: "Tuscarora School board OK's employe (sic) pay increases." My third by-line appeared the day after that, another dry report from another mind-numbing school board meeting, this one in remote Willow Hill. The next day I was back on the front page with an account of the acrimonious contract negotiations between the Chambersburg school board and the union representing school custodians. The story may have lacked sex appeal, but the bitterness of the contract talks was my introduction to just how deeply labor unions were despised in that part of the world.

There were no meetings to cover the next day, mercifully, so I set out on my first enterprise story. At the meeting the previous night, a school board member named D. Eugene Gayman had mentioned, almost in passing, that he intended to step down from the board's presidency at the end of the year. Sensing a story in this, I spent the afternoon reading clips about Gayman and arranged to visit him at his dairy farm for an interview.

As we settled into chairs on the front porch of his farmhouse late that afternoon, it was obvious that Gayman was uncomfortable talking about himself, especially to a reporter. The man was an unvarnished rustic, utterly guileless, and so I took it slow and eventually succeeded in setting him at ease and getting him to talk freely. On that afternoon I made two discoveries: being a reporter opened doors to worlds I never would have been able to enter otherwise; and I had an invaluable ability for a reporter, a gift for getting strangers to open up.

Instead of waiting until Saturday morning to write my story, I headed back to the newsroom, stopping at a greasy spoon for a quick sandwich. As I ate I flipped through my notes, blocking out the story in my head. I was so keyed up I couldn't finish my sandwich.

"The easy smile and the short, rust-colored hair make him look too boyish to be a grandfather," my front-page story began. It then went on to describe Gayman "sitting in a rocking chair as darkness descended on his 170-year-old farmhouse," reminiscing about the changes he had seen in the schools since he first joined a township school board back in 1963. The story wasn't art, but I was proud that I had brought this simple, decent man to life on the page by drawing stories out of him, by painting a scene, by telling his story in clear, unfussy prose.

I'd been on the job one week and already I had taken my first baby steps toward my dream of becoming a novelist. And I was $140 richer.

The All American Rodeo

The following week I took a much bigger step. I rode the fifty miles northeast to Harrisburg in a Jeep owned by *Public Opinion*'s photographer, David Scott Smith, to cover the All American Rodeo out of Weatherford, Texas. We had been promised a whole page for our copy and pictures, and I remember being more than a little on edge about blowing my first big feature assignment. "Journalism," as the British writer Rebecca West put it, "is the ability to meet the challenge of filling space." And a full newspaper page is a daunting chunk of space to fill.

David set me at ease on the drive up to Harrisburg. He was a great talker, quick to laugh, bubbling with energy and enthusiasm. The man could not sit still. The guys in the composing room called him "the free spirit," partly because he neglected to wear socks his first day on the job; he referred to himself, jokingly, as "a brown-haired, blue-eyed Adonis." He did have an eye for the ladies and a very pretty girlfriend who worked in the advertising department, but beneath the mischievous twinkle there was a talented and very hard-working craftsman. David didn't work a mere sixty hours a week, as I had my first week on the job; he worked, literally, 24/7. He had a police scanner in his Jeep, one in the darkroom at the paper, and he slept with one burbling beside his bed.

He was always on call, the blare of emergency codes and the drone of dispatchers comprising the seamless soundtrack of his waking life and his dreams.

He told me a story. One wintry night he'd been awakened by a dispatcher's call for emergency vehicles to respond to a nasty car wreck. But David was battling the flu that night, and he ignored the call, pulled the covers over his head, and went back to sleep. When he dragged himself in to work the next morning, sniffling and miserable, Bob Collins was furious that his staff photographer had slept through a prime photo op—a "fatal"—and he ordered David to get in his car and not come back until he got a picture of the wrecked car. So David tracked it down to a tow lot in Waynesboro and dutifully shot a picture of the twisted mess, which appeared on the front page of that day's paper, the readers unaware of another little subterfuge.

At the rodeo in Harrisburg, David's enthusiasm was infectious. He was a blur, focusing, shooting, reloading, always in motion. He got down in the dirt in the ring, literally under the horses, and I realized he was willing to risk life and limb for a memorable shot. Meanwhile, I was talking to everyone, to an orange-booted cowboy named J. W. Stoker, to an "egg-shaped" organist named Jessie Griffiths, to a first-time rodeo rider named Cindy Price from nearby Shippensburg. This was heaven, this license to go anywhere in the arena and walk up to anyone and just start asking them questions and then writing down what they said. There was a world to be captured inside that building: the barnyard aromas, the organ music and the lights, the costumes, the crowd, the cowboys and cowgirls, the horses, and the bulls. The nature of the rodeo, a series of seemingly random bursts of action with no narrative thread, called for an impressionistic approach in the writing. This was the opposite of hard news. Here's how I described the tools of J. W. Stoker's trade: "Half a dozen lariats are coiled on the floor nearby, as motionless as well-trained snakes. Soon he will charm them to life." Here are the cowgirls: "Some are wearing enormous, tall ten-gallon or Stetson hats. Look at that! One fluorescent blonde just took off her hat and the whole thing must have been stuffed with her teased tinted piled-up molded cone of hair! Hats crammed full of hair! Pink hats, orange hats, powder-blue hats . . ."

Obviously, I was channeling my inner Tom Wolfe, but even then I understood that every writer must pass through phases of mimicry on the way to arriving at his own voice. In the Louvre I had seen students painting copies of the Old Masters. There's nothing wrong with mimicry, as long as it's a learning phase and doesn't become a habit.

The same goes for hyper-ventilating when you write, which is what I was doing when I described the gnarly bulls: "They're all down there. Stamping and stewing and snorting, just waiting for their chance to send some suicidal cowboy into orbit, Gator and Big Bob and Death Valley and Cleburn and Fat Albert, who is positively the ugliest of the entire bunch. There's a huge mound of black flesh knotted between his shoulder blades— what the cowboys refer to, almost affectionately, as 'the launch pad.'"

It wasn't until years later that I learned that Stendahl read a few pages of the bone-dry Civil Code every morning before he sat down to work on *The Charterhouse of Parma* in order to rid his style of what the painter Rackstraw Downes called "the pompous, the pretentious, the grandiose, the overweight." I would learn, eventually, that good writing doesn't need to call attention to itself.

My feature story and David's pictures filled the entire "Family" page the following Thursday. It was the longest, most colorful, most *writerly* thing I'd ever written, a different world from those dry reports of school board meetings, even from the short feature on D. Eugene Gayman. This, I sensed, was the kind of loose-limbed story I needed to write. This could lead to the writing of fiction. This was going to be my launch pad.

In a Strange Land

By the end of my second week on the job it was apparent I had arrived in a strange land. An old joke has it that Pennsylvania is a large state with Pittsburgh on one end, Philadelphia on the other end, and Alabama in the middle. Like all good jokes, this one contains a sizable kernel of truth. Though it's a dozen miles north of the Mason-Dixon Line, and though it stood solidly with the Union during the Civil War, my new home felt more Southern than Northern. It was a world of church steeples, pickup trucks, and manly men who loved to hunt and fish. People ate things like shoofly pie, a viscous confection with a crumbly crust and a high molasses content, guaranteed to clog your arteries faster than wet cement. Also popular was a dubious breakfast meat called scrapple, deep-fried and swimming in—pick your poison—maple or Caro syrup. Volunteer fire departments served as secular churches, providing the stickiest of social glues. Just east of town, for instance, the Fayetteville Volunteer Fire Department held a popular fundraiser every Labor Day weekend that featured ham and bean soup, pumping contests, and performances by the likes of Grandpa Jones and Tom T. Hall. A popular bumper sticker at the time proclaimed that TOM T. HALL *IS* COUNTRY. His anthem was "I Like Beer." The locals loved him.

Few of my neighbors held college degrees, and most of them were white and working-class, distrustful of outsiders, labor unions, liberals, and anything emanating from Washington, DC, which was one hundred miles and several light years away. Chambersburg had its urban touches, including the bustling downtown, some small factories, even a rasty housing project on the edge of town known as Cardboard City, but the place had a largely rural feel—a small town surrounded by carpets of cornfields and orchards, livestock and silos. Sometimes I would round a curve on a back road and have to stop the car because the landscape in front of me was so ridiculously gorgeous I could have sworn it had just finished posing for Grant Wood. This is a section of the long trench that runs southwesterly, between ancient hump-backed mountain ranges, from Vermont to Alabama. Here, between the Susquehanna and Potomac Rivers, it's known as the Cumberland Valley.

This is the periphery of Pennsylvania Dutch country, and every other name in the phone book seemed to end with *–baugh* or *–bach.* People talked funny. If it was raining hard, it was "putting down out." To feed a cow in a fenced pasture, a farmer would "throw the cow over the fence some hay." The infinitive *to be* was frequently dropped, as in, "Bob's lawn needs mowed." And I once heard a man rhapsodize over large female derrières by saying, "The bigger the coosh'n, the better the poosh'n."

Even in downtown Chambersburg the air carried the ammoniac tang of fertilizer and manure. Adding a layer to this heartland ambiance were the ubiquitous Amish and Mennonites, the "plain" people, the bearded men and bonneted women moving along the local roads in horse-drawn carriages or black cars. They were not tourist attractions like the Amish in Lancaster County, where the roadsides were dotted with outlets for Old Amish furniture, apples, clocks, pretzels, and buggy

rides. The Amish and Mennonites in Franklin County lived in the midst of us "English" but stayed very much in their own cloistered world.

One of the more efflorescent daubs of local color was the so-called Peanut Circuit, the two and a half-mile loop in downtown Chambersburg where young people spent weekends cruising in their tricked-out cars and pickups. The starting line was on Philadelphia Avenue at the north end of downtown, and you followed the front straightaway to the town square, where you jogged around the fountain and the Union soldier, then on down to Garfield Street, where you cut left to Second Street, then north up the backstretch all the way to the hairpin turn that put you back on Philadelphia Avenue and the front straightaway. From my modest apartment at the mid-point of the backstretch, I could hear the steady grumble of engines on weekend nights as kids spent hours turning laps on the Peanut Circuit, sometimes drag racing when a red light turned green, echoes of my own youth misspent cruising up and down Detroit's legendary Woodward Avenue.

Of course all those gumball paintjobs and souped-up engines attracted the attention of the police. A retired Chambersburg cop told me that as the 1970s wore on, the beer confiscated from under-age circuit riders stepped up from Pabst Blue Ribbon to the relative sophistication of Coors. The confiscated beer tended to wind up in the confiscating officer's stomach, and a seized keg inevitably inspired an after-hours party for off-duty cops. The cruising got to be such a nuisance that the town fathers cracked down, posting signs at regular intervals along the loop:

NO CRUISING
3 TIMES PAST
THIS POINT
WITHIN 2 HOURS
7:00 P.M. – 1 A.M.

For circuit riders who tired of dodging the cops, there were two drive-in theaters. North of town the Sunset offered lukewarm gore such as *Scars of Dracula* and *Lust for a Vampire*, while south of town the State Line catered to the heavy-breather set with *Swinging Wives*, *High School Fantasies*, and *Keyhole Fest*. Movies didn't get much more B than that.

In spirit, Chambersburg was much closer to faraway Nashville than to nearby Pittsburgh or Philadelphia or Baltimore. People listened to country music and followed NASCAR and Penn State football. They served in the military without complaint and belonged to the American Legion, the Elks Club, the Moose. They appreciated what they had, they did not like change, and they tended to stay put. According to the US Census, Pennsylvania is consistently among the states with the highest percentage of residents who were born in-state, and Franklin County was, and still is, among the most conservative counties in Pennsylvania. In the 1976 presidential election, while Democrat Jimmy Carter narrowly carried the state, Franklin County voted by a margin of nearly 3-to-2 to stick with the dependable Republican incumbent, Gerald Ford.

But I soon realized that through all this stay-at-home, God-fearing, heartland decency there ran a streak of untamable bull-goose lunacy. My first inkling of this was a story circulating in the newsroom that was part of Brad Bumsted's growing legend. It happened before my arrival, while Brad was still earning his spurs as the paper's one-man bureau in Greencastle, south of Chambersburg, just this side of the Maryland state line.

One day Bob Collins got a tip that there had been an epic barroom brawl in Mercersburg, which was in the Greencastle bureau's territory. Collins ordered Brad to start digging. There was nothing on the police blotter about the incident, so Brad called the chief of police, Harry Perrell, who refused to give out any information.

The smell of a cover-up to Bob Collins was like the smell of blood to a shark. Police reports are public information, and he ordered Brad to go back at Perrell, hard. This time the chief slammed down the receiver in mid-conversation. Infuriated, Collins splashed Brad's story about Perrell's stonewalling on the front page.

At that year's Halloween parade in Mercersburg, some supporters of the local police erected a gallows in the bed of a Chevy pickup truck and hanged Brad in effigy, replete with a cowboy hat and a sign bearing his name misspelled as "Bumstead." A sign on the side of the truck urged parade-goers to SUPPORT OUR MERCERSBURG MAYOR AND POLICE DEPARTMENT.

A photographer for a rival paper snapped a picture of the truck with the hanged reporter. The scene has the distinct look of a Deep-South lynching bee: the grinning,

cigar-smoking good ol' boy at the wheel of the hubcap-less pickup, the boy in the flannel shirt with his elbow resting jauntily on the passenger's door, the bearded young man and the boy in the back of the pickup, guarding the dangling dead man under an inky night sky. The scorch of the camera's flash gives it all the lurid aura of a crime scene. The most chilling thing is that this was someone's idea of a joke. Welcome to Alabama.

"That picture creeped me out," recalls Brad, who was unaware of his hanging until he saw the photograph several days after the parade. "But I was young enough and crazy enough that I didn't give a fuck. I was actually proud of it. That's how you make your name in this business."

Bob Collins seemed to agree. A few months later Brad said good-bye to the hole-in-the-wall Greencastle bureau and replaced Rita Meurer, a don't-rock-the-boat, old-school reporter who'd been covering courts and the county commissioners. Collins liked his reporters brash and pushy. Rita was out; Brad was in.

THEN THERE WAS THE LEGEND of Bob Cox, a Chambersburg native who had kicked around at various jobs in radio, in a food-processing plant, and selling cars before getting hired as a reporter at *Public Opinion* in 1959. A few years later, Cox and the paper's photographer, Ken Peiffer, started hearing about strange doings in Shade Gap, a mountain hamlet twenty miles northwest of Chambersburg.

It all started in the spring of 1964. Viola Jacka, a widow who lived alone near Shade Gap, was getting ready for bed one night when a rock crashed through her living room window. Then a rifle barrel poked through the broken glass and a man in a Halloween mask said, "Don't scream, or I'll shoot you." Viola Jacka screamed, and the man fired two shots, one missing her head by inches, the other shattering a nearby flower pot. Viola managed to run to safety at a neighbor's house. The terror had begun.

Two months later, another Shade Gap woman, Anne Weaver, was confronted by a rifle-toting man as she took out the trash. He struck her repeatedly with the rifle as she fled toward a neighbor's house, where she collapsed in the living room, bleeding from a gash in her head. A month later, Martha Yohn was driving home to Neelyton after visiting her sister, her infant son on the seat beside her, when she was startled by logs blocking the road. As she stopped the car, a man materialized on

the embankment beside the road. Though the tempera-
ture was in the eighties, he was wearing a full-length
coat and unbuckled arctic boots. He was also carrying
a high-powered rifle. Remembering the two earlier attacks, a terrified Martha Yohn dropped the car in re-
verse and stomped on the gas pedal. As the car picked
up speed, the bullets started coming, more than half
a dozen, one passing through the windshield, another
shattering the milk bottle the baby was holding. Martha
made it back to her sister's house safely just as the
bullet-pocked car coughed and died.

Now the assailant was given a name: the Mountain
Man. And now Cox and Peiffer, convinced this was becoming a major news story, started making regular trips
from Chambersburg to Shade Gap. They embedded
themselves in the tiny community half a century before
the term came into common use. Like Gay Talese, they
perfected the art of hanging out, becoming part of the
scenery, absorbing information and stories, gradually
overcoming the insular community's innate distrust of
outsiders.

The police seemed powerless to stop the terror. A
mother of two infant children was dragged from her
home and raped. A man had the lower part of his left leg
shot off by the Mountain Man, who, it was discovered,
had spent weeks peering through a bathroom window,
masturbating, as the man's wife took baths. Frustrated
and terrified, the people of Shade Gap started to trust
the two journalists more than they trusted the flummoxed police.

Cox and Peiffer, who had both grown up in Franklin
County, had a working relationship with the cops that
was sometimes nearly jocular. Once, when the journal-
ists approached a police roadblock, state trooper Sam
Kline, recognizing the familiar faces in the car, said,
"Got it solved yet, snoops?"

"Hell yes," Cox shot back, "had it figured out an hour ago, but I'm gonna let you jokers sweat. Wanna make this a really big story."

It became a big story on the day the Mountain Man kidnapped a seventeen-year-old high school junior named Peggy Ann Bradnick as she walked home from her school bus stop. For the next eight days he led hundreds of cops, FBI agents, and gun-toting volunteers on the largest manhunt in the state's history, during which he wounded a sheriff's deputy and killed an FBI agent and a German shepherd tracking dog. Cox and Peiffer were right there, writing and photographing every wrinkle as the drama unfolded.

Finally, on the eighth day, the Mountain Man—who turned out to be an ex-convict and ex-mental patient named William Diller Hollenbaugh, a hermit known locally as Bicycle Pete—was cornered and gunned down. Cox's story opened with typical punch: "The fantastic two-year reign of terror of the Shade Gap Sniper came to a fitting and spectacular end this morning when a bullet from a teenage sharpshooter's rifle snuffed out William Diller Hollenbaugh.

"Hollenbaugh, the deranged 44-year-old native of Dublin Township, Huntingdon County, died in the manner in which he lived the past two years—a hunted man who had lived by the gun and died by the gun."

Peggy Ann Bradnick, traumatized but still alive, was rushed to the nearest hospital and treated for minor bruises, cuts, and blisters. She had not been sexually assaulted. Astonishingly, she was in a forgiving mood, saying,

> It would be easy to say that I despise the memory of him. I don't believe that all the misery, sorrow and death he caused was entirely his fault. It seemed to me that he was a person everybody had rejected. Apparently nobody ever

took an interest in him. He was about as lonely as a human being can get. He was fighting back in the only way he could figure out, trying to capture by force the human companionship that he couldn't get any other way. I just happened to be the one he caught.

Then something even more astonishing happened: Bob Cox was awarded the 1967 Pulitzer Prize in the spot news category. After the judges lauded his "vivid deadline reporting," Cox cried, "I can't believe it! I'm flabbergasted! It's the most unexpected and most fabulous thing that's ever happened to me!" Then, more calmly, he added, "This is my life. I like it. I like to write. I'd rather write than eat."

A decade later, the legend of Bob Cox was part of the oxygen we all breathed in the *Public Opinion* newsroom, a reminder that Pulitzer Prizes don't always go to big papers in big cities, that good stories can come from absolutely anywhere, even from an unassuming, little mountain hamlet like Shade Gap.

AND THEN THERE WAS the strange case of Robert Bear, a prosperous potato farmer in Newville who had been excommunicated by his conservative Reformed Mennonite church in 1972 through a four hundred-year-old practice called "shunning." Bear's sin was to accuse the church hierarchy of lying, an act known as "railing," and he called his ensuing punishment "a living hell of torture." In his book *Pennsylvania: Seed of a Nation*, the historian and anthropologist Paul A. W. Wallace offered this sketch of the practice, which is intended as an incentive for the sinner to repent and return to the church:

Some of the plain sects, in attempting to keep themselves "unspotted from the world," have preserved a number of the medieval customs which they brought with them from Europe and which seem bizarre to modern eyes. The *Meidung,* or "avoidance," for instance, which is practiced by the Amish and others, is said to be one of the cruelest punishments known to anthropologists. When a husband or father (it is usually the man who errs) is "hit with the *Meidung,*" as they express it, his wife is forbidden to eat or sleep with him, and the whole community is under obligation to ostracize him. There is nothing for him to do but, as they say, "go English," which means to leave the community and enter the world of the unsaved.

But Robert Bear was not like most "plain" people, who refuse to sue in court, hold government office, vote, or take up arms in time of war. In an attempt to win back his wife, Gale, and their six children, Bear hired a lawyer to file a suit in Carlisle seeking a court injunction against the practice of shunning. The lawyer advised Bear to get psychiatric and physical exams to prove that he was of sound mind and body. This he did.

Bear then hired Edward C. Michener Associates, Inc., a Harrisburg PR firm, to spread the word about his ordeal. On Monday, July 23, 1973, *Public Opinion* city editor Katy Hamilton received a handwritten mailgram from Clarence C. Smith of the Michener firm. It read: "FYI – *New York Times* sent a reporter-photog team in Friday to see Bear and Bishop Gross." (Bishop Glenn Gross, one of the church elders Bear had railed against, was Bear's father-in-law.) That Monday, the *Times* ran an article under the headline "Mennonite Dissident Shunned by Church and Wife." The reporter, Wayne King, described forty-four-year-old Robert Bear as "the model of raw-boned American Gothic," who was suffering terribly from his excommunication.

"Most painful, however," King wrote, "is that his 35-year-old wife, Gale, who continues in the faith and daily wears the traditional plain long blue gown and cap of the sect, will share neither his table nor his bed and, by Mr. Bear's account, will hardly speak to him.

"His six children no longer have faith and trust in him. He has moved from his farmhouse to a sparse bachelor's trailer. Most of the church, including his father and younger brother, think he is unstable at best. Some think he is flirting with Satan at worst. And much of his farm lies idle because he has been unable to plant the bumper crop of potatoes he has brought forth every year for the past twenty years, earning up to $40,000 annually."

As Bear told the reporter: "The bishops and I are like two stags on a mountain. My wife is the doe standing at the top. A fight is inevitable."

At the very least, Edward C. Michener Associates was earning its fee. But Robert Bear was not content with mere publicity, and so he saw to it that the story shaded from strange to bizarre. Bear hired Probe Detective Agency to look into the "background and character" of J. Henry Fisher, a Reformed Mennonite bishop from Lancaster who had stated that Bear was "disturbed." Anonymous sources told Probe investigators that Bishop Fisher was a "whoremonger" and a "playboy" who entertained call girls in a suite at the Pierre Hotel in New York City, where he also frequented the Latin Quarter and Copacabana nightclubs, tipping the waitresses with silver dollars and squeezes on their fannies. Nothing "plain" about this kind of sporting. Bishop Fisher resigned his church post, citing a heart condition, after dismissing Probe's findings as "bunk."

Brad Bumsted was covering this ongoing soap opera with a mixture of disbelief and dismay. Bear's suffering was real, Brad told me, and it inspired some erratic behavior. One day, after suffering a setback in court, Bear called Brad and asked if he would like to go for a ride. Brad, always on the lookout for a story, agreed. Bear picked him up at the paper and drove him to the house where Gale and the children were living, then he started rummaging in the trunk while Brad sat in the car, wondering what was going on. He watched, amazed, as Bear marched onto the front porch with a sledgehammer and smashed open the locked door. Then Bear hauled three loads of clothing out of the house, put them in the trunk, and drove off.

"Robert, what the hell are you doing?" Brad demanded, realizing he had just witnessed a felony.

"This is a way to get them back," Bear replied.

He was charged with breaking-and-entering and burglary in the incident, and Brad, as he had feared, was subpoenaed as a witness. But Bob Collins stepped in and hired an attorney, and Brad didn't have to testify. A strange land, indeed. Even the "plain" people got themselves into rococo twists.

LAST BUT CERTAINLY NOT LEAST, there was the curious case of Grace Kriner. A woman with a sixth-grade education, she lived in a remote shack surrounded by squalling dogs and dead cars and a lifetime of accumulated junk, where she tramped around in the mud and snow dressed in a gunnysack dress, housecoat, and boots. The area, which doesn't appear on any map, was known as Stringtown. This was beyond Alabama. This was Squalor Holler, Appalachia.

Grace called herself "The Writer," and she produced a column that appeared in *Public Opinion* every Thursday and was as popular with readers as the handiwork of syndicated superstar Ann Landers. A Grace Kriner column was a thing to behold, something Erma Bombeck might have written after a few jars of moonshine. When Grace's handwritten prose arrived in the newsroom each week, a reporter was tasked with typing it up, with strict  instructions not to tamper with the mangled grammar and syntax, the bizarre locutions and medical cures, the rambling thoughts on everything from politics to the weather to the best way to get rid of rats. Reading it, you slipped into a warm Appalachian stream of consciousness. For instance:

> So glad President Ford is enjoying himself now since the elections is over. He can get more rest, not so much on his mind. Take it easy President Ford and family.
>
> Well, it is just about two o'clock on Tuesday morning. Soon fix stoves and lay down to sleep some now.
>
> Got her potatoes and things in the room. Don't want them to freeze so must keep fire going long as she can.
>
> Grace just has her housecoat on now. She surely loves it . . . Grace's both arms surely does hurt her tonight. Course she has drove the car every day this week. No wonder her arms hurt so bad.

And then, out of nowhere, comes a crystalline nugget of political analysis:

> But I do believe that if President Ford wouldn't have pardoned Nixon he would of had a better chance of staying in as president. Do think that did hurt President Ford a lot. You see, the people before did not vote President Ford in in

the first place, only ex-President Nixon did put him in office then President Ford soon gave Nixon a pardon. So it didn't look too good after all.

Grace and her grizzled husband, Harvey, lived off Social Security and the weekly check from *Public Opinion*. She referred to him as "Grace's Man" and "The Writer's Man," and I developed a suspicion that Harvey might have been prone to get a little too deep into the sauce. One morning Grace needs to drive a friend to town for a 9:00 a.m. doctor's appointment, hardly an early wake-up call for people in places like Stringtown, Pennsylvania. When Grace's car won't start, a neighbor tries to roust The Writer's Man from sleep, without luck. Was he sleeping off a snootfull? Then one night Grace's Man—drunk?—starts a fire inside the shack:

> Mr. Kriner had a terrible accident at home. It was a bad thing that did happen. They could have been homeless by now as fire is a bad thing at any time.
> Mr. Kriner was burned pretty bad on both sides of his face and his eyebrows burned, too, and his right arm, also. But he has learned a lesson never to put cold oil in a stove again.
> Grace will not let him make any fire no more. It made an awful noise when it blow up. It could of set the house on fire. But thank God it didn't. But it did burn his shirt some.

But perhaps The Writer's greatest achievement was her medical advice, with its strong whiff of backwoods voodoo:

> They say if a child has asthma bore a hole in an upright post. Put a piece of the child's hair in the hole and close the hole with a peg. This must be done at sunrise.

If a child has whooping cough put a caterpillar in a thimble, tie it in an oilcloth sack around the child's neck. He will recover more quickly.

A reporter hanged in effigy. A deranged and murderous Mountain Man. A shunned Mennonite. A newspaper columnist living in rural squalor worthy of William Faulkner or Carson McCullers. It went from strange to stranger to stranger yet. But the strangest was still to come.

The Journalists and the Murderer
And the Lawyer and the Dog

In tight spaces—submarines, prisons, small-town newspaper city rooms—people tend to make fast friends and even faster enemies. David Scott Smith and I had hit it off on our trip to Harrisburg to cover the rodeo, and at my insistence he started teaching me how to shoot pictures with one of his spare Nikon 35-millimeter cameras—the mysteries of f-stops, depth of field, focus, and shutter speed. Reporters were encouraged to take their own pictures, because it lightened the load on over-stretched David and, in the bargain, saved Gannett money. I didn't mind. I loved taking pictures and was delighted to discover that I had a decent eye.

Brad Bumsted became another fast friend and an informal mentor without either of us quite realizing it. After our double by-line from "Garden City, New York," on my first day, I took to studying Brad—the way he talked on the phone, the kinds of questions he asked, his different registers, from flattering to pleading to bullying. I realized he would stop at nothing to get a story, and get it right. He relentlessly double-checked himself, made the extra phone call, never hesitated to ask stupid or prying or annoying questions. He had no interest in being liked, and he refused to be outworked. He taught me to butter up secretaries, the gateway to many news sources. Most important of all, he reinforced the lesson Bob Cox had taught us: since good stories can come from absolutely anywhere, your radar has to be turned on at all times.

My apartment on the backstretch of the Peanut Circuit was just a block from the town square, so Brad and I started meeting for breakfast at Palmer's Drug Store, across the street from the courthouse. We pored over out-of-town newspapers while we ate big, greasy breakfasts, getting jacked on coffee, listening to the chatter of the regulars. Those breakfasts taught me the importance of gossip and eavesdropping, two things that until then had seemed more than a little unclean. They are neither. They are vital sources for every writer.

Maybe Bob Collins sensed the growing bond between Brad and me, or maybe he thought I'd gotten off to a fast start. For whatever reason, after my second week on the job, Collins handed me a plum assignment: he wanted me to travel with Brad to Easton, Maryland, to write sidebars while Brad covered the testimony in the murder trial of Merle Unger. If it wasn't the trial of the century, it was big news to the readers of *Public Opinion*, and it was guaranteed to put us on the front page for the coming week.

Merle Unger was a local legend. He'd grown up in Greencastle, one of twelve children of a carpenter father and stay-at-home mother, a family on speaking terms with the notion of rural poverty. By the time Merle was old enough to drive a car legally, he was well down the road to a life of crime. His first arrest was in 1967, when he was seventeen, on a gun-theft charge. His court-appointed lawyer was the Franklin County public defender,

Blake Martin, a booziferous dandy and raconteur who freely admitted that cocktail hour was his favorite time of day. The kid criminal and the lawyer clicked.

Petty criminals are hardly a rarity in small-town America, and in those years, his apprentice years, Merle's offenses were minor—car theft, breaking and entering, joy riding, nothing special. But during one of his extended stays at the old Franklin County Jail, the Georgian pile that had somehow escaped the flames when the Rebels torched the town in 1864, Merle exhibited his true genius for the first time. On at least half a dozen occasions, he and a fellow inmate broke out of jail after lights-out and went out for a night on the town, visiting girls, playing bingo. Then they broke back *into* the jail before deputies counted noses in the morning. This went on until the night a deputy was playing bingo and looked across the room and was startled to see a couple of faces he recognized from inside the jail.

Merle Unger, it turned out, had a rare gift. He was an escape artist, a hillbilly Houdini who combined tremendous physical strength with astonishing ingenuity in his mission to prove that no cage could hold him. In May of 1975 he became the first person to escape from the new, state-of-the-art Franklin County Jail, which sprawled behind razor wire-topped cyclone fences out past the interstate. While cutting a fellow inmate's hair in the prison yard, Unger slipped through a door left open by a guard who was escorting a prisoner. Merle smashed a window, dropped to the ground outside the fence, and was gone. He made his way to a hideout in nearby York, Pennsylvania.

It was beginning to become apparent that Merle Unger was much better at breaking out of prison than he was at staying out of prison. Or as a former state trooper put it, "He's an expert at escape, but he's not too damn good at staying escaped." From his hideout in

York, Merle wrote a letter to his girlfriend, who was in prison on a robbery conviction. Apparently hoping she would write back, Merle included his return address on the envelope. It wasn't long before the York police came knocking, and Merle was back in jail. It's almost enough to make you think he *wanted* to get recaptured so he could escape again. Escaping was the whole point, after all, and you can't escape if you're already escaped.

This time Merle stayed on the inside for a total of three hours. He squeezed through a gate into the recreation yard, scaled a twelve-foot, chain-link fence, ran across a roof, and dropped back into the free world. Four months later, he and a girlfriend were caught robbing an ice cream store in Carlisle, and this time Merle got sent to the Cumberland County Jail.

The Legend of Merle Unger had now reached full gallop. What's not to love about a bad boy who doesn't merely thumb his nose at authority but makes the authorities look foolish and inept? Don't we all wish we could do it—stop being solid, by-the-book burghers and just *bust out*? Apparently, Merle had tapped into some deep, unspoken yearning, because an informal fan club coalesced. T-shirts began to appear. "Merle, Baby, Where Are You?" asked one. "Run, Merle, Run," urged another.

On December 4, 1975, Merle and another inmate overpowered a guard in the Cumberland County Jail, erected a forty-foot-tall stack of tables and chairs in the prison cafeteria, climbed it, smashed through a skylight, scrambled onto the roof, and vanished. Nine days later, the Legend of Merle Unger stopped being the stuff of light farce.

A LITTLE AFTER NINE O'CLOCK on the evening of December 13, 1975, Merle Unger walked into a Hagerstown, Maryland, grocery store called Kim's Korner. He was wearing a blue ski mask and carrying a .25-caliber pistol. Two women were at the counter buying beer when Merle pointed the gun at the man behind the register, Russell Sheppard, and demanded all of his paper money. After Sheppard emptied the cash register, Merle ordered him to empty his pockets. Sheppard handed over a thick wad of bills. Merle started for the door, almost $4,000 richer than he'd been when he entered the store.

But there was a snag. A man had come in off the street while Merle was holding the gun on Sheppard. Donald "Barney" Kline was a regular customer, lived just up the block. He was also an off-duty Hagerstown police officer, and he was carrying his department-issue .38-caliber pistol. As the robber neared the exit, Kline shouted, "Stop! Police officer!"

Merle kept going, and Kline followed him out the door with his .38 drawn. Sheppard followed the two men and found them struggling in a nearby alley. Then Sheppard heard gunshots and saw Unger run away as Kline staggered out of the alley and collapsed. "Get me some help," Kline gasped. "I've been hit bad."

Forty-five minutes later Kline was pronounced dead from three .25-caliber gunshot wounds to his chest. A K-9 German shepherd named Snoopy led police to Merle Unger, bloody and unconscious, in a nearby cellar. He'd been shot twice—once in the chest, once in a forearm—but his wounds were not life-threatening.

After that, as Brad put it, the attitude around Chambersburg was "no more fun and games about Merle Unger."

On May 14, 1976, three days before his murder trial was scheduled to begin, Merle broke out of the Washington County Detention Center in Hagerstown, Maryland. A month later he tripped a silent alarm during a burglary of a cocktail lounge in Orlando, Florida, and police found him hiding under a table. That afternoon, as he was being transferred in handcuffs from the Orlando Jail to the Orange County Jail, Merle bolted from a police car, rolled under a gate, and led police and a dozen pedestrians on a foot race through downtown Orlando. A public-relations man named George Haberkern eventually got Merle in a headlock until police arrived. Steve Paulson, a reporter for *The Orlando Sentinel* who had joined the chase, said, "This guy could really run. He ran just like a turkey."

Unger's trial had already been moved once. Now, in light of the fresh publicity from events in Florida, a judge granted a defense request for a second change of venue, and the trial was moved to Easton, Maryland, a small town on the Eastern Shore, about 125 miles from where Barney Kline was murdered.

And so on the Sunday before Thanksgiving, the eve of the trial, I climbed into the Buick with Amos beside me in the front seat and Brad and Blake Martin in the back, and we rolled. Blake was not Merle's attorney for this trial. That honor went to the Hagerstown public defender, Joseph Padula, but Blake was hoping to write a book about Merle, and he wanted to sit at the defense table, gathering material, available if Padula needed any help. On the way to Easton, the boys in the back seat chain-smoked and pounded beers, getting loud and merry. Blake told us that he and Merle had asked the fabled defense attorney F. Lee Bailey to take on the case, even offered book or movie rights to Merle's story as compensation. Bailey wrote back to say he was busy defending Patty Hearst.

By the time we made it to Easton, the guys in the back seat were lit up like a couple of ocean liners. Our odd, ten-legged menagerie checked into a double room at the cheapest motel in Easton, a Gannett-mandated economy. Brad and Blake each took a queen-size bed, while Amos and I slept on the floor, serenaded by drunken snores.

THE NEXT MORNING I SAW Merle Unger in person for the first time. He was much smaller than I'd expected, almost scrawny, with dirty-blond hair that was obviously not going to be with him much longer. But Merle's physique and his thinning hair were not my story. His hardware and his escorts were my story.

Merle had arrived at the Talbot County Courthouse accompanied by two carloads of state police, state penitentiary officers, sheriff's deputies, and plainclothesmen. One carried a sawed-off shotgun. Merle's hands were cuffed in front of him, and his ankles were linked by a short chain. He would not be running like a turkey, or anything else, on this day.

Shortly before the noon deadline, I roughed out a story in my notebook, then phoned it in to the newsroom. This was a new experience, talking a story instead of writing it. I noted that Merle "minced" his steps as he left the white sedan that had brought him to Easton from his maximum-security cell at the Maryland State Penitentiary in Baltimore, where he was serving a ten-year sentence for the Hagerstown escape. He would be returned to his cell in Baltimore every night for the duration of the trial.

Everett Foreman, the chief deputy in the Talbot County Sheriff's Department, told me he thought the local jail could hold the wily Unger. "I think we can handle him," Foreman said, "but I'm glad we don't have to."

MOST OF THE SPECTATORS CROWDING the courtroom were cops. Though they were off-duty, they wore their uniforms as a show of solidarity with their fallen brother, Donald Kline. It was obvious they had come here for blood. They spent the trial glaring at Merle Unger, their eyes ablaze with murderous loathing. When word got around that Brad and I were bunking with one of the cop killer's lawyers, we felt the heat of those stares.

On the second day of the trial I wrote a meatier story about how the lead prosecutor in the case had persuaded the two local newspapers to keep a lid on pre-trial publicity until the jury was in the box. He didn't want to give the defense any ammunition for another change of venue request—and the loss of what appeared to be a slam-dunk conviction in a high-profile case. Such convictions tended to come in handy at election time. The papers happily complied.

On the final day of the trial, I faced the test that makes or breaks every journalist. When a small woman with black hair came into the courtroom and sat in the back row, I failed to notice because I was busy sketching Merle and his two lawyers. Brad nudged me. "That's Merle's mother," he whispered. He didn't need to say more. I knew I had to interview her.

I can still recall the two emotions that went to war inside me. As I studied Mildred Smith Unger, I felt the reporter's adrenaline rush that comes with knowing I had a good story, a good, exclusive story; I also felt a stab of doubt, a sense that it would be cruel and cold, that it would be *wrong*, to walk up to a stranger and start asking her questions while a jury debated whether or not to lock her son up for the rest of his life.

As the testimony wound to a close, I kept glancing at the woman. She showed nothing. She might have been waiting for a bus. Meanwhile, the war raged inside me. I couldn't do this. I had to do it. It was immoral. It was necessary. It was wrong. It was my job. I would hate myself if I did it. I would hate myself much more if I didn't do it.

I knew that if I didn't do this I would never make it as a journalist or, most likely, any kind of writer. As the jurors left the room to begin their deliberations, I was paralyzed

When Merle Unger's mother stood up, Brad gave me a look. That was all it took. I followed the woman out of the courtroom.

I caught up with her in the courthouse lobby, gazing out a window as the daylight drained from a gray sky. I introduced myself and took out my notebook and started with small talk, as I'd done with D. Eugene Gayman on his farmhouse porch. Mildred Unger told me she had fifteen grandchildren and "the sixteenth is due in January." She told me that she chops the wood that heats her house, a house that sits alone on the side of a mountain, surrounded by woods and open spaces. I detected the first drop of bitterness when she told me her husband is a carpenter who has "fixed everybody's house but mine," and that she never learned to drive, preferring to stay at home. "Besides," she added, sounding resigned, "my husband believes that's where I belong."

I didn't ask why her husband hadn't accompanied her to the courthouse. Instead, I worked the conversation around to her son. She expressed a mother's predictable feelings of shock, denial, and empty hope. "Sure, I was surprised when I heard what Merle did," she said. "But I've always thought he wouldn't do something like that unless somebody did something to him first. And we still don't know exactly what happened."

It wasn't hard to fight off the urge to say *Oh yes, we do, we know exactly what happened.*

As the jury's deliberations entered their second hour, I remarked that she seemed surprisingly calm, given the circumstances. "People tell me I should get more excited about things," she said. "I guess it's the Smith in me that keeps me calm." My story ended with this:

A commotion at the top of the stairs signaled the jury's return to the courtroom. She took one last look at the sky, then said: "You know, I've always been a firm believer that there's more good than bad in life."

Then she climbed the stairs and took her seat in the back of the courtroom. When the jury delivered its verdict – guilty on all counts – her eyes remained dry and fixed on her son.

I had passed the test. At a later hearing, Merle Unger was sentenced to life plus forty years.

LONG BEFORE I INTERVIEWED Mildred Unger, I had read Joan Didion's 1968 masterpiece of reportage, *Slouching Towards Bethlehem*, which contains this truism: "Writers are always selling somebody out." Years later I read Janet Malcolm's nonfiction book, *The Journalist and the Murderer*, which opens with famous lines that amplify Didion's sentiment: "Every journalist who is not too stupid or too full of himself to notice what is going on knows that what he does is morally indefensible. He is a kind of confidence man, preying on people's vanity, ignorance, or loneliness, gaining their trust and betraying them without remorse."

Malcolm nailed it. I felt no remorse after I finished interviewing Mildred Unger. One reason for this is that though she was stoic and taciturn, natural tendencies that were surely magnified by the ordeal she was undergoing, she made no effort to repel or evade me. Quite the opposite. She was willing, if not eager, to talk. I have experienced this willingness many times since that day, and I'm still trying to unravel the mystery of it. Why are people who are facing the most horrific circumstances— disaster, death, prison, the loss of a loved one—so willing to talk to reporters?

Janet Malcolm offered a theory:

> Something seems to happen to people when they meet a journalist, and what happens is exactly the opposite of what one would expect. One would think that extreme wariness and caution would be the order of the day, but in fact childish trust and impetuosity are far more common. The journalistic encounter seems to have the same regressive effect on a subject as the psychoanalytic encounter. The subject becomes a kind of child of the writer, regarding him as a permissive, all-accepting, all-forgiving mother, and expecting that the book will be written by her. Of course, the book is written by the strict, all-noticing, unforgiving father.

In *Speedboat,* her weird little novel published around the time of Merle Unger's murder trial, Renata Adler has her protagonist, a journalist, muse on this very question:

> I used to wonder why the victims of some small sensational tragedy—the parents of a little girl who had just been thrown from the roof of her tenement by a deranged older boy, or the family of a model son who had just gone clear out of his mind and murdered a friend—never shut the door in my face when I came for an interview. They never do. They open the door; they bring out the family album and the baby anecdotes. I used to think this was out of a loyalty to memory, or a will to have the papers get it right. I still think it's partly that, and partly being stunned by publicity and grief. But now I know it's mostly an agony of trying to please, a cast of mind so deep and amiable that it is as stark in consciousness as death.

Now we're getting somewhere: *childish trust and impetuosity . . . an agony of trying to please . . .*

These counterintuitive impulses, it turns out, are not confined to unsophisticated country people like Mildred

Unger. The renowned photographer Sally Mann is no-body's idea of a yokel, and yet she exhibited her own streak of childish trust and impetuosity in 1992, when *The New York Times Magazine* sent a writer named Richard B. Woodward to interview Mann after she'd published a controversial book called *Immediate Family*, which included sixty pictures of Mann's three pre-pubescent children going about their lives, sometimes without clothing, on their remote Virginia farm. Writing in the same magazine in 2015, Mann recalled,

> During the three days of interviews at my home, I was a sitting duck, preening on her nest without the least bit of concealment. So I can hardly fault Woodward for taking his shots at me. In my arrogance and certitude that everyone must see the world as I did, I left myself wide open to jour-nalism's greatest hazard: quotations lacking context or the sense of irony or self-deprecating humor with which they were delivered.

Then Mann flipped the equation. Having been stung as the subject of a journalistic interview, she wondered what drives the subjects of her own photographs to be so open. "(H)ow can they be so willing?" she asked. "Is it fearlessness or naïveté?"

Mann doesn't answer her own questions, but she does admit that the uproar inspired by Woodward's article caused her "furious pain." On top of the pain, for good measure, there was a dollop of self-recrimination: "That it was essentially self-inflicted made it all the worse."

These counterintuitive impulses—trust, impetuosity, arrogance, fearlessness, naïveté, an ache to please—are surprisingly common, and they go a long way toward relieving journalists of the queasiness that comes with the essential immorality and coldness that lie at the heart of their enterprise. These impulses also explain why so many people despise and distrust journalists. *I let him in so close,* Sally Mann and others say after the fact, *and then he went and cut my guts out.*

THAT NIGHT, POLICE OFFICERS and attorneys for both the prosecution and the defense convened in an Easton restaurant for a booze-fueled celebration of the guilty verdict. As always, Brad and Blake and I sat apart from the others, eating our food and drinking our beers, tolerated by the gleeful throng but in no way welcome to become a part of it. Not that we wanted to. It was not that we sided with Merle Unger; it was that this merriment seemed like an inappropriate way to honor a fallen comrade. It was so vulgar and cheap.

As the liquor continued to flow, I looked across the room and noticed that Joe Padula, Unger's lead attorney, was sitting at a table full of cops, and he was pie-eyed, roaring at someone's joke. As I watched, Padula laughed so hard he rocked back on his chair's hind legs, then his hands started paddling the air as he lost his balance and pitched over backwards, hitting the floor with a room-rattling *thwomp!* I could see Padula's wingtips wiggling in the air above the table. There was a moment of stunned silence, then the place exploded. Men shouting, laughing, banging the tables with fists and glasses. *That goddam Joe Padula!* As cops helped him to his feet, I was scribbling in my notebook, getting it all down. This time there was no stab of doubt or self-loathing like I'd felt as I approached Mildred Unger. This was the unalloyed thrill of knowing I had a knockout story. I would show readers how the judicial system really works. Cops and DAs and public defenders all in bed together, having a ball. *That goddam Joe Padula!*

By the time Brad and I left the restaurant, Padula was back in his chair, and the decibel level had gone back down. I noticed that Blake was still pounding down drinks, but he didn't look happy like everyone else in the room. He looked like someone at a wake.

THE VERDICT WAS RETURNED late Wednesday afternoon, well past deadline. Since *Public Opinion* didn't publish on Thanksgiving Day, Brad and I decided we would spend the night in the Easton motel, then drive back to Chambersburg in the morning and write our stories there in time for the noon deadline on Friday.

Brad and Amos and I were awakened before dawn by a string of strangled curses coming from the vicinity of our room's twin sinks, which stood outside the bathroom door. In the harsh fluorescent light we could see Blake Martin, dressed in his pajamas, holding a toothbrush. He sounded like he was dying, spitting furiously into one of the sinks, gulping water, cursing, spitting.

"Blake, what the fuck?" Brad moaned.

When Blake came up for air, he mumbled, "Was dark. I reached for the toothpaste but accidentally picked up the goddam tube of Preparation H!"

The lawyer went back to rinsing and cursing while the journalists and the dog tried to go back to sleep.

BRAD AND I WROTE our stories in the deserted newsroom on Thanksgiving Day and showed up for work late on Friday morning. My interview with Mildred Unger ran on the front page under Brad's lead story about the guilty verdict, which was embellished with my first published drawing—a crude but passable likeness of Merle Unger, Blake Martin, and Joseph Padula at the defense table during the trial. My joy at this double coup didn't last long. My account of the post-verdict revel and Padula's drunken spill was not on the front page—or anywhere else in the paper. When I asked Katy Hamilton what happened to it, she gave me a frosty look and told me Bob Collins wanted to see me. Right now.

On the way to Collins's office, I tried to figure out what could have gone wrong. Did I fuck something up? Impossible, I told myself. My story was solid, easily the best thing I'd written so far. Or maybe I was trying to reassure myself because I didn't want to let Collins down. He was one of those rare editors who had a gift for making reporters want to outdo themselves. Not because we feared him, but because for some unknowable reason it was important to win his approval. His approval was like a warm bath; its flipside, as I was about to learn, was a shocking cold shower.

I took a deep breath and rapped on Collins's door. He waved me in. As soon as the door closed behind me, even before I could sit down, he roared, "What the *fuck* were you thinking?"

I didn't have to feign shock. I sputtered, "What do you mean, Bob?"

He slapped the printout of my story like he wanted to hurt it. "This, this . . ." It took him a moment to find the word. "This piece a *shit*. What were you trying to do, get us sued out of existence?"

"Sued?"

"Have you heard about these things called libel suits?"

"Of course."

"You write a story about a defense attorney getting drunk with a bunch of cops after his client is convicted of murder, and you don't think he'll sue us?"

I didn't know much about libel law, just two things. First, you can't libel the dead; and second, you can't get convicted of libel if you can prove that what you wrote is true. Since Joseph Padula was still above ground, to the best of my knowledge, I decided to go with defense number two. "But Bob," I said, "it happened exactly the way I wrote it. Brad was sitting there with me. Ask him."

This redoubled Collins's fury. "Quit being so fucking naïve! The cops'll back Padula up when he denies it. Who you think a jury's gonna believe, the cops or a couple of wise-ass reporters?"

I couldn't think of anything to say to that. Collins waved me out of his office and told me, in so many words, to get my head out of my ass.

I walked back to the newsroom in a fog, crestfallen. My first big assignment had turned into a cluster fuck, but I tried to tell myself that I had learned several things worth knowing. I'd learned that the fact that something happened does not automatically make it fit to print. There are many factors lurking in ambush, including the risk of a libel suit (even if something is true), the capacity to hurt feelings and damage reputations, the possibility of appearing unseemly or cruel. This newspaper happened to be in a small town, where everybody knew everybody, and, therefore, slights were magnified, less easy to pardon or forget than they might be in a faceless big city.

All that was worth knowing, but I had learned something far more valuable. My encounter with Mildred Unger had taught me that being a reporter may be morally indefensible, but I was willing and able to gain people's trust and then betray them without remorse. I had no problem selling people out. As I sat down at my desk, still stinging from Collins's rebuke, I consoled myself since I had passed a major test. The trip to Easton taught me I had the right kind of blood, the cold kind, to make it as a reporter.

A Buck's Revenge

On the Monday after Thanksgiving the two-week buck hunting season opens in Pennsylvania. I was unprepared for the psychic magnitude of this event, because I'd grown up in Detroit, gone to college in a New England city, and lived in California, where I never saw a deer hunter, never saw a dead deer lashed to a car fender, never saw a man peel the hide off a tree-hung deer carcass like it was a stubborn patch of indoor-outdoor carpeting. All that changed in Chambersburg.

In Franklin County—in much of rural Pennsylvania, in much of rural America—the opening of buck season is a hallowed moment, a siren call to don the camo and the blaze orange, fill up the flask, load the rifle, and head off into the great outdoors. Schools and many businesses in Chambersburg and surrounding towns closed on the Monday after Thanksgiving, an acknowledgement that just about nobody would show up to work or shop. It almost felt like a religious holiday. In a sense, it was.

The gong went off at seven o'clock that Monday morning, and within minutes the woods and fields were booming with gunfire. Within hours the parade began. Proud hunters who had bagged their buck would pull up to the loading dock at the rear of the *Public Opinion* offices, then pose for a picture with their inert, glassy-eyed trophies. If David Scott Smith wasn't available, reporters and other staffers filled in to snap these obligatory gore portraits, an autumnal staple in the paper. The captions that accompanied these pictures were clinical, as dry and factual as a police blotter:

> These two hunters were among the earliest in the state to bag deer Monday as the two-week buck season began at 7 a.m. Lewis Shank (left), R.R. 1, New Oxford, shot a 9-point, 122-pound buck with a 16½-inch spread. Its longest tine was 7¼ inches. He shot it at 7:09 a.m. using a 6.5 magnum Remington rifle.

We reporters tended to be college educated, usually from a faraway city—Washington, DC, Philadelphia, Bangkok, Detroit—and most of us took a dim view of this vaguely pagan blood sport. David Scott Smith summed up our sentiments: "What I objected to was the mindset of the hunters, the buck fever, the macho thing. Guys walking down the street saying, 'Didja git yer buck yet?' For the most part these guys weren't like the DeNiro character in 'The Deer Hunter.' It was more like the American drunk with a gun."

One night, possibly inspired by the contents of our own flasks, David and I decided it was time for the bucks of this world to push back. David had a friend named Kevin Armstrong who managed a downtown clothing store called the Ram's Horn, which had a trophy head of a big-horn sheep mounted on the wall. It wasn't a deer, but it had horns, and that was good enough for our purposes. We took it down and tied it to the driver's headrest in a VW Beetle. Then Kevin sprawled on the hood, and David and I lashed him in place with a rope. I think I splashed ketchup on Kevin and the car, but I can't remember for sure. David then snapped a roll of pictures that did, indeed, make it look like the antlered

one had turned the tables and bagged himself a human trophy. I thought of it as *A Buck's Revenge*.

It was such a brilliant spoof that we absolutely had to share it with the world. I must have already overcome my post-Easton tongue-lashing, because the next day David and I walked into Bob Collins's office and showed him the contact sheet, urging him to run one of the pictures in the paper with a straight-faced caption like the dry and factual ones that ran under the gore portraits. Collins smiled briefly, thinly, then gave us a look that said he wanted to have us committed. He didn't even have to ask the questions: *Do you have any idea what the people in this county would do if they thought we were mocking deer hunters?* And, *Do you have any idea what would happen to our circulation numbers? And our ad revenues?* The questions hovered in the air unasked, their answers understood by all. With a shake of his long-suffering head, Collins ordered us to get back to work.

There was, after all, news to report. On the opening day of buck season that year, nearly a million hunters took to the woods and fields in Pennsylvania. Ten of them wound up dead before sundown: seven suffered heart attacks, one suffered a fatal stroke, and two, the youngest two, died in ways too prosaic and predictable to qualify as tragedy. According to the *Associated Press*:

> Authorities say Wayne Robert Thompson, 12, of Farrell in Mercer County, was hunting with his father and friends Monday near Four Corners in Elk County.
>
> He was about 150 yards from his father when he spotted a deer, gave chase and fell. His rifle discharged and the blast struck him in the head.

And:

> Mark Allen Shatz, 14, of St. Marys in Elk County, was shot once in the head by fellow hunter Earl Renner, 45, of Perkasie in Bucks County, police said.

And:

> Thomas Kabusk, 46, of Trumbull, Conn., shot himself in the chest while climbing a tree to hunt near Wilkes-Barre, authorities said. He was hospitalized in critical condition at Nesbitt Hospital, Kingston.

For the first time, though not the last, I thought, *Get me out of this place.*

What an Asshole!, Redux

One of the many reasons I barely squeaked through college was that instead of taking notes during classes, I usually spent the time drawing. Doodling might be a more accurate word for what I was doing. Trying to capture the faces of my professors and fellow students, maybe a hand, a leg, a stack of books, the tree outside the classroom window. I was largely self-taught, having taken only one art course in my life, a drawing class taught by the inspiring Edward Koren, whose whimsical cartoons of hairy critters have been appearing in *The New Yorker* for decades. I became a wind-up toy, my pen in constant motion.

Courtrooms are even more boring to me than classrooms, so as I sat listening to the drone of testimony during Merle Unger's trial, my pen started dancing again. Seeing my drawing of Merle and his lawyers in print, with my by-line, must have felt even better than getting my back scratched by Marilyn Monroe, because soon after returning from Easton I wound up in another courtroom, this one in the Franklin County Courthouse, sketchbook in hand, drawing another local man who was on trial for murder.

My new subject was Alan Lee "Pede" Scarborough, a twenty-four-year-old from Mercersburg, the town where Brad was hanged in effigy and where I'd covered the Tuscarora school board meeting my first night on the job. Scarborough was accused of shooting his best friend, Russell Douglas Straley III, in the head with a .45-caliber automatic pistol. Scarborough told police he and Straley had had sex and then argued about politics before Straley's death. Scarborough also claimed he was a cat named "Panda" and that he had become "possessed" after members of a motorcycle gang left a rock with white feathers inside it at his birthday party three years earlier. He claimed the rock had "supernatural importance." He also believed his telephone was tapped, and the government knew everything about everybody. This last claim sounded reasonable enough to me, but a clinical psychologist testified during the trial that Scarborough was schizophrenic, and his attorneys were claiming he was not guilty by reason of insanity. The local strain of bull-goose lunacy was back in the news.

Now comes one of my more spectacular lapses of memory. I have zero recollection of attending that trial or drawing the accused killer. But for some reason I had clipped my drawing of Scarborough from the paper and saved it, and it's now sitting on my desk, badly yellowed with time. When I happened upon the undated drawing in a box of old clips, I had to go back to Chambersburg and scroll through microfilm to ascertain that the drawing appeared on the front page of the December 7, 1976, edition of *Public Opinion*, along with Brad's article about the trial. My drawing shows bearded Pede Scarborough sitting at the defense table, his head hanging, his eyes peering down into the abyss that awaits him: conviction on a charge of third-degree murder, followed by a long prison sentence.

My discovery of that long-forgotten drawing reminded me that there are only a few things I know about writing. One is this: When a writer finds a subject and puts out his antennae, when he makes himself available

to information and insights about his chosen subject, things will find him. There might be something slightly magical about this, but there's nothing remotely coincidental. I'm not sure that's the same as saying these discoveries are pre-ordained, or fated; but they're definitely not coincidental. Maybe these discoveries are meant to be, maybe not. But I do know that, for whatever reason, that drawing of Pede Scarborough spent nearly forty years buried in a box, and then it found me at the precise moment I needed it.

But that's not the only example of something finding me. Shortly after I started writing this book, I visited a magazine editor in New York, looking for freelance work. As we talked, my eye landed on a short stack of magazines on the floor of the office. The picture on the cover of the magazine on top of the stack showed a naked couple under rumpled bedclothes in a tacky, brass bed. The man, balding and bearded, sports a gold chain, a hairy chest, and visible rolls of blubber. A real swinger. For some reason, instead of smoking a post-coital cigarette, he's talking into a microphone that's attached to a bulky tape recorder. The woman, a poor man's Farrah Fawcett, has the bedclothes pulled up to her armpits as she primly types something on an electric typewriter. The picture screamed 1970s to me, specifically soft-core '70s porn. Intrigued, I read the headline above the brass bed: *Kiss & Tell Journalism*. It wasn't a porno mag, after all, it was the January 1977 issue of *MORE: The Media Magazine*. Beneath it were half a dozen more issues, ending with March 1978. Amazing. These magazines spanned, almost to the day, my tenure at *Public Opinion*.

I'm convinced those magazines found me because I had made myself available to them. It was like the completion of an electrical circuit. The editor agreed to let me borrow the magazines, and I read them in a state of rising excitement. I had vague memories of reading *MORE* back in the '70s, and these back issues brought back many things, including the stories that were making headlines back then: Rupert Murdoch's controversial purchase of *The New York Post*, celebrity journalists, UFO magazines, CIA payments to journalists, the aforementioned *Kiss & Tell Journalism*, *The Washington Post*'s ruthless campaign to bust its unions. The major advertisers were makers of booze and cigarettes, staples in every self-respecting journalist's diet in those days. The articles were sharp and opinionated, by the likes of Garry Wills, Murray Kempton, Alexander Cockburn, Dwight Macdonald, and Nicholas von Hoffman. Above all, the articles served as a reminder that in the 1970s, journalism mattered to the national life in a way it no longer does. In our post-newspaper, atomized Internet age, it's hard to imagine anyone fretting that the liberal *Washington Post* was actually anti-union, or that news sources and reporters were getting a little too chummy, or that the TV news anchor Barbara Walters was pulling down a million dollars a year.

ONE OF THE PEOPLE I tracked down while writing this book was Maude Scott, who was a rival reporter in Chambersburg and is now managing editor of *The Daily Journal of Commerce* in Seattle. One of the first stories Maude told me on the phone from Seattle was the stunning news that she was also in the courtroom during Pede Scarborough's murder trial, and she was also sketching the accused.

This was so, Maude explained, partly because she had attended Mercersburg Academy with Pede, but mainly because she was then a cub reporter in the two-person Chambersburg bureau of the nearby *Waynesboro Record Herald*, where her editor was Bob Cox, whose reporting for *Public Opinion* had won a Pulitzer Prize in 1967. The Scarborough trial was big news.

One night during the trial, Maude told me, she was drinking in a downtown Chambersburg bar, maybe the Elks Club, when I walked in. Like the trial and my drawing, this encounter is gone from my memory. Maude recalled that I recognized her from the courtroom and approached her at the bar with a "proprietary" air, hinting that she was poaching on my turf by sketching in the courtroom. *What an asshole!* I thought, not for the first time.

But Maude didn't let my churlishness—childishness?—put her off. And though I don't remember our encounters in the courtroom or at the Elks Club, I do remember being attracted to this striking, young woman with a curtain of blond hair, big lively hazel eyes, and hints of dimples when she flashed her electric grin. We soon discovered we had things in common besides our shared love of drawing. We were about the same age (she was twenty-one, I was twenty-four), we were both new at our jobs, flying blind, and more than a little insecure. We loved a lot of the same writers, Sherwood Anderson, Joan Didion, James M. Cain, Flannery

O'Connor, Hemingway's Nick Adams stories. She also had a silky-coated bird dog, a Gordon setter named Sarah. She even drove a big, fat, old car, a pea-soup-green '52 Chevy she'd bought from Bob Cox for $125. Sarah and Amos hit it off. So did Maude and I.

Soon Maude introduced me to her bureau-mate, a fast-talking eccentric named Tom Kelchner who had an elfish mop of hair and a goatee, a taste for fine wines and a passion for photography. In Chambersburg, Tom passed for an eccentric, a rare and welcome commodity. He'd rigged up a darkroom in the upstairs bathroom of the duplex apartment where he lived with his wife Beverly, across North Third Street from the *Public Opinion* offices. Tom taught me how to develop and print photographs, and he and Beverly made no secret of their scorn for the townsfolk, who they regarded as a bunch of blinkered yahoos.

While I have no recollection of my first meeting with Maude, I vividly remember the first time we made love. It happened in the upstairs guest bedroom of the Kelchners' apartment, while they were away for a weekend and Maude and I were house-sitting, along with our dogs. I remember that the room was chilly, and the light was silvery that day, and I still remember how effortless it was to fall in love with gorgeous, talented, brainy Maude Scott. Some things, it turns out, are impossible to forget.

Gun to the Head

A mos had a new playmate, I was falling in love, and I loved my new job. Every morning I hurried through the pre-dawn darkness to Palmer's Drug Store to meet Brad for breakfast. Then at 7:30 sharp, jacked to the gills on bad coffee and adrenaline, we sat down at our red Selectrics and pounded for the next four and a half hours. It wasn't unusual for a reporter to produce half a dozen by-lined stories before noon.

It was the ideal way to learn how to write: with a gun to your head. Writer's block was not an option. Speed was a goal, of course, but it was not enough. Accuracy and clarity were kings as we sweated to fill the allotted space, no small challenge since we were feeding a beast that could never be satisfied, that had to be fed anew, from scratch, every day. We were like athletes developing muscle memory, only instead of trying to replicate an action—like, say, a basketball player shooting a free throw—every action had to be different. No two sentences could be identical. So as I began writing each sentence, my mind was already jumping ahead to how the sentence would take shape, how it would end, how it would feed into the next sentence and then how the paragraph would end and feed into the next paragraph. Words were a river that never stopped flowing. I was learning to control the flow, steer it, shape it into narratives that had to be instantly graspable. If I made a mistake—a typo or a false start or a wrong word—I would cross it out with a black, felt-tip pen so the scanner wouldn't pick it up when my typed story was fed into the editor's computer. This archaic system cut down on false starts and carelessness. As soon as I finished one story, I reached for a fresh sheet of red-bordered copy paper, cranked it into the machine, and started the next. I was in heaven.

But I also had a problem. Ever since I'd acquired Amos as a pup in the summer of '72, when I was working at the Vermont horse farm, we had gone everywhere and done everything together. The dog had worn a leash a total of once: the time we rode a ferry where all dogs had to be restrained. I had to take off my belt and improvise a leash for the forty-minute boat ride.

Amos was so well trained that he would sprint along the sidewalk in a busy city while I rode a bicycle in the street, and if he beat me to the corner he would sit and wait until I gave him the signal that it was safe to cross the street. He accompanied me to all my outdoor jobs and all my classes when I returned to college. The only times we were apart for extended periods were when I was working a split shift in the kitchen of a San Diego restaurant. I'd rented a room in a big house with half a dozen roommates near Windansea Beach, and while I was at work my roommates kept Amos amused. Between my lunch and dinner shifts I took him down to the legendary surfing beach at the end of our street, where he would sight a covey and sandpipers skimming along the waves and give chase. I would watch him turn into a black speck, then vanish. A few minutes later the black speck would reappear, growing larger, chasing a fresh covey in the opposite direction. He gave me a heads-up as he passed, and soon disappeared again. Eventually, he returned, exhausted and sopping, and I took him home and left for my dinner shift. When I got home late at night, Amos was always waiting inside the front door, ecstatic at my return.

My newspaper job meant I had to leave him alone for long stretches of time, either in my apartment or in my car. He was clearly unraveling under these unfamiliar forced separations, barking, acting jumpy. Sometimes when I walked home from work late at night I could hear him howling inside the cage of my apartment. Something had to give.

One day I arranged to interview the new principal at Corpus Christi, the Catholic school on the north side of downtown. After lunch I swung by the apartment to pick Amos up for the short walk to the school. When we got there I commanded him to lie down outside the door and "Stay!" He knew the drill. He'd done it hundreds of times without a leash.

The nun I interviewed that day was perfectly pleasant, but the experience was the worst kind of déjà vu. I was stunned to see that she was wearing the habit of the Immaculate Heart of Mary sisters, the very nuns who had taught at Holy Name School outside Detroit, where I attended first through eighth grades. This nun wore the same upside-down U-shaped cardboard helmet, covered by the same black veil, with the same patch of white cloth covering her hairline. The same semi-circular breastplate supported the same high, stiff collar. The same long-sleeved, blue gown flowed to the floor, concealing everything but hands and face, completing the job of neutering the woman. The habit discombobulated me so badly, at first, that I had trouble asking the nun questions and writing down her answers.

Memories were bombarding me. Memories of attending Mass every morning before school, the drone of Latin and the smells of beeswax and incense, singing in the boys' choir, the sting of classroom rulers on knuckles, the incessant harping about sin, the breakfast treat of glazed donuts and orange juice on the Fridays we received Holy Communion, which, for some unfathomable reason, had to be preceded by a three-hour fast. That Immaculate Heart of Mary nun in Corpus Christi School brought it all roaring back, the hocus pocus, the discipline, the low fever of terror, the relentless campaign to make us believe that just about everything we did, especially the things that felt good, were a one-way ticket to the ovens of hell.

When I finally escaped that nun and stepped out into the dying afternoon, Amos was gone. I called and whistled. Nothing. This had never happened before, but I was too rattled to be worried. I figured he got bored and walked home, so I walked home. But he wasn't waiting for me there, and I felt the first whisper of worry.

I walked the downtown streets for an hour, whistling, calling his name, but there was no sign of him. I went back home to make dinner, figuring he would show up.

When he had still failed to show by the next morning, my worry shaded toward panic. Maybe I should call the dog pound, or post LOST DOG signs around the neighborhood. When I got to work, Bob Collins overheard me talking about Amos, and, to my surprise, he became acutely, almost aggressively, interested in my dog's disappearance. It turned out Collins's wife bred Irish Setters, and he had a soft spot for dogs. He asked if I had a picture of Amos, and I remembered that one of the first pictures I had successfully printed in Tom Kelchner's makeshift darkroom was a shot of Amos sitting on the floor and giving the camera a quizzical look, his blue right eye sparkling. Collins sent me home to fetch a copy, and when I returned he ordered the guys in the composing room to work up a LOST DOG classified ad using the picture. Since I didn't have a telephone at home, I included the Kelchners' phone number with the picture. Collins didn't charge me for the ad.

When I stopped by the Kelchners' apartment that night to see if anyone had called, Tom gave me a stricken look and said a man had called and left a call-back number. Numb with dread, I dialed the number. I don't remember the man's name, but I do remember that he identified himself as a veterinarian, and he told me that late the previous afternoon, which was when I was interviewing the nun at Corpus Christi, he was walking to his car in the parking lot of Farmers & Merchants Bank, which was half a block from my apartment, directly on the way back from Corpus Christi School. As he was getting into his car, the vet said, he saw another car back up and hit a black-and-white dog that was trotting across the parking lot. The vet hurried to the scene.

He told me the dog, which looked very much like the dog in the newspaper ad, was badly hurt and obviously in pain. There was no way to save him, the man said, so he drove him to the Animal Shelter and saw to it that he was humanely destroyed.

I thanked the man and hung up the phone and left the house. I spent that long night walking the empty streets, trying to swallow the fact that my boon companion was gone and life as I had lived it for the past four and a half years was now turned upside-down, changed forever. I couldn't get it out of my head that the nun at Corpus Christi had been a harbinger of doom, like a crow or a loaded gun in the opening chapter of a bad novel. I tried to convince myself that it was a blessing to know for sure what had happened to Amos, that is, *if* the man who claimed to be a veterinarian was telling the truth. I chose to believe he was for the simple reason that I couldn't bear to live with the thought that he was not. Yes, the loop of uncertainty, of not knowing what happened or, rather, not being able to convince myself that I knew what happened, would have been too much.

Work saved me. I don't know that I'd ever worked as hard as I worked in the weeks after Amos's death. *Not* working was the problem. Maude was a true comfort, but the absence of Amos in my apartment became a kind of cruel presence. I couldn't bear to be alone in the place with his ghost.

So I found a new apartment, a three-story townhouse a few blocks south on Second Street, and Brad agreed to move in with me. The high-ceilinged rooms were echoingly empty, even after we'd furnished them with our bachelor scraps. We had no television, no telephone, no stereo, so to brighten the place up I dragged home a toilet bowl from a curbside trash pile. It sat in the living room next to the nubby brown sofa, our idea of a conceptual sculpture. Brad had an 8-track tape player and a collection totaling two tapes, *Al Green's Greatest Hits* and *Rags to Rufus*, featuring Chaka Khan. They became the monotonous soundtrack inside our man cave. *Tell me something good, tell me that you like it . . . Times are good, times are bad, and what's happy is sad . . .*

To make the grim scenario absolutely perfect, our landlord was a mildly retarded local man who pestered us incessantly about making sure we kept our stove light in working order and didn't allow pigeons to roost in the eaves. He regularly announced his plan to coat the building's exterior with a pigeon repellent called No Roost, but he never delivered on the promise. Brad and I derived a perverse joy from his frequent visits to the apartment.

Whenever people asked me if I planned to get another dog, I just shook my head. The question struck me as absurd, tied to the fantasy that everything in life is replaceable, reproducible. Amos's death was a seismic event. On one side of the crack was my carefree, footloose youth, its odd jobs and vague dreams and cross-country trips, now utterly gone; I was standing on new ground, grown up, on my own, out making my way in the world, and I understood there was no looking back. I have never owned another pet.

Winter roared in, and with it came a whole new level of weirdness.

PART TWO

A Death In the Family

The Psychic

On December 3, 1976, a distraught mother in Waynesboro, Pennsylvania, wrote a letter to Salvatore Lubertazzi, a police detective in Nutley, New Jersey. It read:

Dear Detective Lubertazzi,

I read in a newspaper about Mrs. Dorothy Allison helping you with a case in 1975. She helped find two children. I was wondering if you could please help me get in touch with her to help me find my daughter.

She has been gone since July 22, 1976. Our police can't find anything. It will soon be five months, and I and my family are nearly out of our minds.

Her name is Debbie Kline. She was nineteen on November 28. She disappeared coming home from work. We found her new 1976 Vega parked in the mud and thick bushes. Her pocketbook and all her ID cards were in her billfold, along with $30.

Please help me if you can. I don't know what else we can do. Please call me collect anytime.

Please do not think this is a prank or anything like that.

Please, please help me. I have no place else to turn, and it is terrible when you try and try and find nothing. Please help as soon as possible.

Thank you very much.

Mrs. Richard Kline Sr.

I knew these rudimentary details about the disappearance of Debbie Sue Kline, because *Public Opinion*'s Waynesboro reporter, Marie Lanser, had been covering the story with pit-bull doggedness. As the Christmas holidays approached, the case was almost five months old and growing colder by the day. The police, as Mrs. Richard Kline noted in her letter, were baffled. The initial torrent of newspaper articles about tips, dead-end leads, a prayer service, search parties involving a helicopter, bloodhounds, scuba divers, and the National Guard had dwindled to a trickle. I was too busy dealing with Amos's death and stories of my own to take much notice. The Debbie Sue Kline story meant almost nothing to me.

To Marie Lanser it meant everything. An Army brat who'd finished high school in Bangkok and then majored in history at Wilson College in Chambersburg, Marie had worked as a summer intern and stringer for *Public Opinion* before getting hired full-time in June 1976, shortly after her college graduation. A month later, Debbie Sue Kline disappeared, and Marie, at age twenty-two, was plunged into her first big story. It soon consumed her.

She paid frequent visits to the missing girl's parents, Dick and Jane Kline, trying to develop a rapport with the couple she came to regard as "sweet country people." But Marie was playing against a stacked deck. The pair covering the story for *The Waynesboro Record Herald* were my girlfriend's boss, the Pulitzer Prize-winner Bob Cox and his collaborator on the Shade Gap story, Ken Peiffer. Both men had grown up in the area, and they had two lifetimes worth of contacts in and out of law enforcement. But Marie was no pushover, and she was undaunted by the competition, which she described as "gracious and cordial, but fierce."

Marie Lanser had a delicate beauty that masked a tough interior. While writing about skydivers, she'd strapped on a parachute and jumped out of an airplane. In order to gain first-hand knowledge of the sport's physical jolts, she'd climbed behind the wheel of an old beater and competed in a demolition derby at the Fulton County Fair. To research a series about over-the-road truckers, she'd hopped into the cab of an 18-wheeler in Hagerstown and ridden all the way to Atlanta and back, the CB radio yammering non-stop. But on the Debbie Sue Kline story, no amount of moxie could hide the fact that Marie was operating at a horrendous disadvantage.

As Ken Peiffer put it, "Bob and I were at the Klines' house just about every day. We were locals, born and raised here. For an outsider to make inroads and contacts and build trust—that takes a long time. The Klines were trying to keep the story alive in the paper, but the story died off after a while. Then someone told Jane Kline about Dorothy Allison."

Jane Kline wrote her letter to Detective Lubertazzi. Then Dorothy Allison agreed to come to Waynesboro. That's when I, and a lot of other people, started to sit up and really take notice. This story was about to go way beyond the old bull-goose lunacy, all the way to a new place I have come to think of as the land of psycho-horror.

DORTHY ALLISON WAS A PSYCHIC. She was cooking sausages in the kitchen of her Nutley, New Jersey, home when Sal Lubertazzi, who screened her voluminous correspondence, hand-delivered Jane Kline's letter. Allison had been having visions since she was a girl, and by late 1976 she had helped police on more than one hundred cases. She did not accept money for her services. On the day Allison received Jane Kline's letter, she received another plea for help from another mother whose daughter had disappeared on the very day Debbie Sue Kline vanished. Allison knew the instant she touched Jane Kline's letter that the woman's daughter was dead.

After serving a hearty Italian meal to Detective Lubertazzi and his wife, Allison told them, "I'm going to Waynesboro, maybe before Christmas. I can help find their daughter for them."

The spookiness had begun.

DORTHY ALLISON, IN PRELIMINARY phone conversations with Jane Kline, Cox, and Peiffer, started riffing on some of the things she was seeing:

> I see two men involved . . . their names are Ronald and Robert or Richard, I'm not sure about the second one . . . I'm looking for a man whose middle name is either Lee or Leroy . . . there will be double letters in the last name of one of the men . . . there should be a high hill . . . and I see a line of some kind . . . one of the men has a knife . . . one of the guys is already in jail, but it's for something else. . . .

Finally, she told Jane Kline, "I feel something very important is going to happen around the thirteenth of January. I'm not sure what it is, but in the end, it will make sense."

Much of what Allison was saying was mystifying to the parents and the reporters. As Peiffer would say later, "So many of the things Dorothy said you could put together in hindsight, but putting it together when she said it was very hard to do."

Sometimes it was impossible. But hindsight would show that her visions started coming true even before she arrived in Franklin County. On January 13, 1977, the day Allison had singled out to Jane Kline, police arrested a man named Richard Lee Dodson and charged him with attempting to rape a twenty-six-year-old housewife near Ft. McCord, northwest of Chambersburg.

Dodson, who owned an elaborate criminal résumé, had a wolfish look about him with his Brylcreemed hair and gun-nut sideburns. Marie Lanser wrote a straight news brief about Dodson getting arrested and locked up in the Franklin County Prison in lieu of $10,000 bail. She quickly forgot this minor news item. Though no one realized it at the time, the first piece of the Debbie Sue Kline puzzle had clicked into place.

DELAYED BY SOME VICIOUS WINTER storms and by work on other missing-person cases, one of them in Florida, Dorothy Allison finally arrived in Chambersburg by car on a frigid Saturday, January 22, nine days after Richard Lee Dodson's arrest. The many hours Cox and Peiffer had spent cultivating a relationship with the Klines now began to pay off. Allison's first stop was at Cox's home. He and Peiffer then drove her to Waynesboro Hospital, where Debbie Sue Kline had been employed in the cafeteria. The psychic toured the building, trying to pick up visions. She correctly identified the door Debbie Sue Kline had used to exit the building on the day she disappeared, as well as the first name of the woman Debbie had relieved in the cafeteria. Watching her, Cox thought of a bloodhound being primed with a scent.

In the hospital parking lot, they were joined by a plainclothes state trooper and three friends of the Kline family, all of them openly skeptical of the psychic's purported powers. The three-vehicle caravan proceeded to the spot, less than two miles away, where Debbie's abandoned Vega was found. Riding in the unmarked police car, Allison then guided the caravan northwest. Cox turned on a tape recorder as Allison slipped in and out of a first-person monolog, switching from present to past tense, sometimes seeming to speak in the voice of the missing girl: "I went from one place to another. I'm not in the same town I started in. I know that. As far as the distance goes, it's not clear. But I went to another place . . ."

Allison asked the men questions, but she ignored their answers. She was receiving more pictures.

"As I talk about it," she went on, "I get the feeling of sharp instruments. I hear a sound. I thought it was a voice. A very funny sound I hear. Yes, like knives. I'm seeing something like a knife."

Later, as the caravan moved through the desolate winter landscape, she blurted out, "I don't know why, but I get this feeling about a shoe. It's a dark shoe, but that could be because it's dirty. Remember that. The shoe is very important."

Four days later, the trooper at the wheel of the cruiser would understand the importance of the shoe.

When the caravan crossed the Maryland state line, Allison shivered and adjusted the hood of her bulky parka. A sudden chill told her they were going in the wrong direction, so the caravan turned around and headed back across the Mason-Dixon Line into Pennsylvania.

"I don't know, these crazy people are animals," Allison said, wincing as she received an especially appalling picture. "These crazy people know where to hide somebody. I see a dump . . . She's halfway in and halfway out, not completely buried. Not deep. And she's a virgin."

Daylight was fading. The weary caravan headed back to Chambersburg.

THE POSSE RECONVENED the next morning, and the tour of the area continued. By now Allison referred to the killers as Ronald and Richard, she knew they both had extensive criminal records. One had raped his own daughter, and it was possible that one of them was in the Franklin County Prison. "I see lots of twin things," Allison said. "Everything I see in this case is double. I see doubles in their names and in the place where she's buried."

She saw other pictures in her mind. Images of junk-yards and dumps, the color yellow, the word "burnt," swimming pools, a muddy shoe. At 1:30 that afternoon, Allison predicted there would be an attempted prison break that day. A little more than three hours later, a sixteen-year-old inmate choked a matron and tried to escape from the Franklin County Prison.

Allison then visited the Klines' home, where she touched various pieces of the missing girl's clothing, including her favorite pair of blue jeans, the dress she wore to her recent high school graduation, and the out-fit she was wearing when she had her senior picture taken. Allison slipped the girl's school ring on her fin-ger, then rubbed her hands across the girl's bed sheets, which had not been changed in the six months since her disappearance. Allison explained that physical con-tact with personal articles frequently triggered images.

The home tour complete, Allison left for New Jersey shortly before dark, saying she would undergo hypnosis after she got home. She promised she would be able to identify the car used in the abduction, its license plate number, the names of the people involved, and Debbie Sue Kline's location.

AFTER SPENDING THE WEEKEND with Allison and getting eight hours of her musings on tape, Bob Cox, predictably, produced a riveting scoop on the front page of Monday's *Record Herald*. Debbie Sue Kline was back in the news.

Cox's story opened with Allison's accurate prediction of the attempted prison break. A sidebar detailed the psychic's track record, including her prediction nearly a decade ago that Robert F. Kennedy was in danger from "a dark-skinned foreigner" shortly before he was assassinated in 1968 by Sirhan Sirhan. "But perhaps the best-known effort by Mrs. Allison," Cox wrote, "was her vision of seeing Patty Hearst, San Francisco, Calif., in the farm home in Pennsylvania prior to the time Miss Hearst was rescued from her Symbionese Liberation Army captors. Mrs. Allison informed the police and the FBI that they could find Miss Hearst in Pennsylvania on a rural farm. Police verified that Miss Hearst had indeed lived in the farm house and left only days before they arrived on the scene."

Allison made an audacious new statement: "She also predicted for the *Record Herald* that she would solve the disappearance of Miss Kline."

Blindsided by these stories, Marie Lanser produced her own front-page story about Allison's visit in the next day's *Public Opinion*, based on interviews with the Klines and unidentified police sources. Marie followed that a day later with a story about Allison's visit to the Kline home, which included another prediction, this one from Jane Kline: "She's going to find (Debbie). Maybe not the way we want her, but she'll find her."

The Franklin County Prison was now buzzing with talk about the psychic. She had correctly predicted the attempted prison break, according to the papers, and she had vowed to name Debbie Sue Kline's abductors. The consensus among the inmates was that she was a cinch to solve the case.

One inmate begged to differ. "They think they know about it, but they don't," Richard Lee Dodson told his cellmate. "Not a goddam thing. It's a lot of hogwash, all that stuff in the papers. It's a big bluff. Do you hear me? A bluff!"

The startled cellmate had no idea what Dodson was talking about, but the police had been hearing things about Richard Lee Dodson, all of them bad. A reward was being offered for information in the Kline case, and this inspired the predictable flood of crank calls. But some of the information was starting to make sense. One tipster claimed he'd been drinking with a guy named Ronald Henninger, who bragged that he'd killed a man in Illinois and said he liked to check out the "young chicks" who worked at Waynesboro Hospital. The cops knew Henninger: he was wanted for raping his daughter, who now, at age eighteen, was married to Henninger's cellmate from an earlier prison stretch, one Richard Lee Dodson. Henninger was also wanted for raping the fourteen-year-old stepdaughter of his current wife, Barb. But Henninger had vanished.

The next tipster arranged a barroom meeting between Barb Henninger and an undercover cop who posed as a cousin of Debbie Sue Kline. Barb Henninger told the cop that her husband was back in jail in Illinois for parole violation. She also said that before his recent arrest on the attempted rape charge, Dodson had come to her complaining of nightmares, visions of blood running down Debbie Sue Kline's blouse. Dodson told her that he and Henninger had kidnapped and raped the girl, then Henninger had slit her throat.

It was intriguing, but it didn't rise above the level of hearsay, and it wasn't nearly enough to get arrest warrants on Henninger or Dodson. The cops needed a body.

THE COMPETITOR IN MARIE LANSER couldn't bear to get scooped. So after filing her story for the Wednesday paper, she fired up her '75 Chevy Monza and sped more than two hundred miles to Nutley, New Jersey, where Dorothy Allison welcomed her like "royalty" even though the two women had never met.

Allison told stories about her "gift" as she served a lavish meal that ended with fresh strawberries for dessert, an unseasonal luxury on that cold January night.

"She was this jovial Italian housewife," Marie recalled recently, "but there was definitely hocus pocus there. She had a powerful something."

At one point Allison said, "You have four letters in your name."

Marie started to protest before remembering that since her wedding just six weeks earlier, her married name did indeed have four letters. "That gave me pause," Marie said. "When she started to tell me about my future, I told her to stop. It was impressive to be so close to a psychic. It was humbling."

In the course of the evening, Allison got a call from her police contacts in Pennsylvania. They told her there had been a break in the case. Late that morning, an inmate in the Franklin County Prison had agreed to lead police to Debbie Sue Kline's body—after admitting that he and Ronald Henninger had kidnapped and raped the girl, but insisting it was Henninger who had killed her. The prisoner then guided two carloads of state troopers up Burnt Cabins Road to the top of Fannettsburg Mountain, on the Huntingdon County line. They parked near a large, yellow sign that marked the telephone right-of-way across the mountain. The prisoner led them to a dump in the woods and said, "This is the place."

After handcuffing the inmate in the back seat of one of the cruisers, the cops spent an hour dusting away snow and turning over debris in the dump. There were no signs of a body. Finally, they agreed to un-cuff the prisoner and bring him down to the dump. He lifted up a piece of debris and smiled. The troopers looked down and saw a dirty, white shoe, a bone, and the pant leg of a hospital uniform. It was the skeletal remains of Debbie Sue Kline.

The cops put the prisoner, Richard Lee Dodson, back in cuffs and returned him to the cruiser. When they called Allison to tell her the news, they made her promise not to reveal the suspects' names to the press until they were ready to file formal charges. After she got off the phone, Allison told Marie she knew the names of the two suspects and would reveal them if Marie promised not to print them until the police filed charges. Marie agreed. The name Ronald Henninger meant nothing to her, and at first she didn't recall writing a news brief about Richard Lee Dodson getting charged in the attempted rape in Ft. McCord.

The parallels between Allison's earlier visions and actual events were too numerous to ignore. She had seen a junkyard, the color yellow, the word "burnt," a muddy shoe, a knife, double letters, a man with the middle name Lee.

Only later, when she was on the phone with Bob Collins, did Marie realize that her promise to Dorothy Allison had put her in a sticky predicament. "I told Collins that Dorothy had given me the name of the killer," she said, "and that she asked me not to reveal it. And I was going to honor her confidence." Part of Marie's motivation was her respect for Allison's psychic powers. "I said to Collins, 'I can't tell you. If I do, she'll know.'"

The newspaperman on the other end of the line was not pleased that one of his reporters was withholding such a major scoop. "Collins," Marie said, "was furious."

Now here's something refreshing, something you don't see every day, something that goes against the claims about journalists made by Joan Didion and Janet Malcolm and countless others. Here was a reporter who refused to sell out a source, a reporter whose word of honor was more important to her than a scoop.

Marie's story about her visit with Allison, with no mention of Henninger or Dodson, appeared on Thursday's front page under the tip-toeing headline "Psychic sees confession in Kline case by tomorrow." Below Marie's story was a short article by staffers under a bland headline: "Body found in Fannettsburg." The banner headline in the *Record Herald* was much stronger: "Body believed that of Debbie Kline." The decomposed body needed to thaw before an autopsy could be performed, and police refused to speculate on its identity or release the names of any suspects.

On Thursday, Marie hurried back to Chambersburg. When she got to the newsroom late that afternoon, reporters and editors crowded around her desk, pumping her for details about her encounter with the psychic. I don't recall being in the newsroom when Marie made her triumphal return from New Jersey, but, as writing this book has taught me, that doesn't mean I wasn't there. Marie, however, has vivid memories of the scene.

"I learned a valuable lesson from Bob Collins that day," she said. "He walked into the newsroom and cut through the crowd around me and said, 'Don't talk. Sit down and write.' My job wasn't to tell my story. My job was to write it." Wise advice for anyone who has talked away a book in a barroom.

Marie's front-page story on Friday dealt with the tug-of-war Allison frequently got pulled into by skeptical police departments. Allison had insisted all along that she didn't solve crimes; she merely helped police, who then closed cases. The police in Pennsylvania came off as less than grateful for whatever help she'd provided in solving the Kline case. "To the best of my knowledge, she hasn't aided us," said state police Sergeant Ray Hussack. Allison shot back, "No one can tell me I did not play a significant role." As for police downplaying her contributions, she said with a shrug, "I'm used to it."

By then, an autopsy had confirmed that the remains discovered in the Fannettsburg dump were those of Debbie Sue Kline, and the cause of death was "hemorrhage from a neck wound." Though the police weren't saying so, Dodson's statement claimed that after he and

Henninger had taken turns raping the girl, Henninger had slit her throat, then they covered the corpse with a blue, plastic swimming pool. Afterwards, they sat in Henninger's Mercury Cougar and cracked open a fresh round of beers. "Well, Dodson," Henninger said, "now you know what a cold-blooded bastard I really am."

On February 9, Marie Lanser's secret finally got out. Ronald Henninger and Richard Lee Dodson were formally charged with the rape and murder of Debbie Sue Kline.

DID DOROTHY ALLISON SOLVE the case? We all puzzled over that question in the newsroom. Marie, who was closer to the story than the rest of us, still has strong feelings about the answer. "I think that case was going nowhere," she said recently, "and then Dorothy comes to town and the case cracks wide open. Dodson saw the newspaper articles, got spooked, and spilled his guts to his cellmate. Then he started blabbing to the cops. You could make the case that if she hadn't gotten involved in the case, it's my guess that no one would have ever known what happened to Debbie Sue Kline. Her body would still be up in that landfill."

The story hasn't left Marie. She still lives just outside of Waynesboro with her husband, Ed Beck. Their two daughters are grown now and gone, but when they were younger Marie admits she was an "uber-protective mother," refusing to let them walk the half-mile to school without an escort. Though she and Ed live on a bucolic hilltop, with three of his brothers as their nearest neighbors, Marie still insists on keeping her car doors and the house locked. She ignores the frequent teasing that she's being paranoid.

"Covering that story was creepy, because I didn't know the landscape," she says. "One day I followed the route Debbie drove every day from the hospital to the

Klines' house. The first time I drove along that curving stretch of roadway, I thought it was one of the most beautiful drives I'd ever taken. Then the horror of her being kidnapped there, then the unspeakable murder. I could never reconcile the disconnect."

She has a hard time explaining the disconnect to people who don't know about the shadows that punctuate the lovely landscape.

"People come here from out of town and say, 'What a beautiful area.' And I say, 'Yeah, but the first big story I covered here was the kidnapping, rape and murder of an eighteen-year-old girl.' It shook me to the core."

The Ninth Guy
on the Bench

The Debbie Sue Kline story shook me, too. The Mountain Man, the shunned Mennonite, Grace Kriner, buck fever, the Peanut Circuit, the hillbilly Houdini turned cop killer—all that was strange, but somehow manageable. The Debbie Sue Kline story, on the other hand, was a tick too American Gothic. This was not boilerplate insanity, or local color, or eccentricity. This was pure evil at loose in the world, an echo of the small-town and backwoods horrors found in *In Cold Blood* or a Flannery O'Connor short story. Then, for good measure, a psychic comes on the scene from a place called Nutley and four days later a jailbird confesses to a grisly crime that had stumped the police for six months. This was too much.

So I kept my distance from the Debbie Sue Kline story, which was easy to do, because it was clearly Marie Lanser's turf. Besides, I was off writing feature stories about interesting nobodies, including a survivor of Legionnaire's Disease, a retired Navy pilot who became a successful portrait painter, and a Hagerstown taxidermist who mounted a little bit of everything, from deer heads to Alaskan sheep, antelope, wild turkeys, a toy poodle, and a Chihuahua. He even made an ashtray out of a moose's foot.

I came to think of the subjects who interested me as the Little People, and I use the adjective with unapologetic irony. For a long time I worried that I was guilty of a fatal lack of ambition for not being more interested in the Big Important People, and that this would keep me from making the big time. But there was nothing I could do about it. I realized my attraction to idiosyncratic, marginal subjects flowed from my aversion to canned news and the pack journalists who covered it. This was the aversion I'd first exhibited during my job interview with Bob Collins, when I'd opted to report for work the week after the presidential election.

Eventually, I realized this inclination was not a liability, and it actually put me in good company. Years later, while reviewing the collected sports writing of venerable Gay Talese, I noted that he was drawn not to star athletes but to the people who worked the margins of the sporting world—boxing referees, timekeepers, horseshoe makers, midget wrestlers.

Alison Lurie compared Charles Baxter's fiction to Alice Munro's with words I regard as high praise: "Baxter is also like Munro in the way he treats all levels of society as of equal interest and value. For him the personal history and internal psychological and moral life of a hospital nurse are just as important and complex as that of a highly educated lawyer or doctor."

In reviewing a biography of the journalist Joseph Mitchell, Charles McGrath wrote, "If he could help it, Mitchell never wrote about anyone who was famous or newsworthy. He was drawn to people on the margins: bearded ladies, Gypsies, street preachers, Bowery bums, Mohawk steelworkers, the fishmongers of the Fulton Market." Mitchell, McGrath added, "was genuinely interested in his subjects as human beings, remarkable because they so vividly demonstrate that one way or another we are all a little weird." Mitchell took this a step further. In the foreword to his collection *McSorley's Wonderful Saloon,* he wrote, "There are no little people in this book. They are as big as you are, whoever you are."

G. K. Chesterton believed that one of Charles Dickens's chief virtues was his "democratic optimism," meaning Dickens was convinced that everything, and everyone, is potentially interesting. David Foster Wallace seemed to agree. "Early in 2008," recounts the essayist and frequent *GQ* contributor John Jeremiah Sullivan, "*GQ* asked [Wallace] to write about Obama's speeches or, more largely, about American political rhetoric. It was still a somewhat gassy idea as presented to him, but Wallace saw the possibilities, so we started making inquiries to the Obama campaign, and even made reservations for him to be in Denver during the convention. Our thought was to get him as close to the head speechwriters (and so as close to Obama) as possible. But Wallace said, very politely, that this wasn't what interested him. He wanted to be with a worker bee on the speechwriting team to find out how the language was used by, as he put it, 'the ninth guy on the bench.' It also seemed like maybe a temperament thing, that he would be more comfortable reporting away from the glare."

This has always made perfect sense to me—wanting to write about the ninth guy on the bench, and being more comfortable reporting away from the glare. Why? It may be a temperament thing, but more likely it comes from understanding that it's so hard to get a stranger to open up to you, and it's so scary to crawl inside a person if they do open up to you, that you're wise to get rid of as many impediments as possible. And one of the most forbidding impediments is that glare Wallace so wisely avoided. Whenever there are bright lights, clusters of cameras and microphones, handlers and spin doctors and packs of hungry rivals with notebooks, the reporter's chance of getting something unique, or merely genuine, all but evaporate.

Or maybe this is somewhat gassy in its own way. Maybe it's as simple as this: I have interviewed hundreds of rich and powerful and famous and self-important people, but few of them were half as interesting to me as that Hagerstown taxidermist who made an ashtray out of a moose's foot.

ON THE DAY DEBBIE SUE Kline's remains were discovered, I had two by-lined stories in the paper. One was a feature about the Pulitzer Prize-winning Washington columnist Jack Anderson, spawn of Drew Pearson, who taught me that claiming not to be self-important can be its own kind of self-importance. Yes, thank you, Jack, *that's* the point. There's nothing inherently wrong with being rich or powerful or important or all of the above. The killer is *self*-importance.

Anderson had come to Gettysburg to speak to a packed ballroom at the Sheraton Inn on a subject that interested me not at all: the Book of Mormon. But Anderson was a famous syndicated Washington columnist, and we couldn't always afford to be picky about the stories we covered. So off to Gettysburg I went.

In a "swooping and soaring" voice, I wrote, Anderson portrayed life in Washington as "secret combinations of criminal intrigues of wicked people who operate behind closed doors." That sounded plausible. The rant continued, "When we reach that fullness of iniquity we will be swept off, unless we repent."

This was the same doomsday drivel I heard every morning at Palmer's Drug Store, at meetings of the Kiwanis Club, at conclaves of local pols' fretful constituents. The crowd in Gettysburg spooned it up.

Anderson was obviously aware that railing against that snake pit known as Washington would play well out here in the sticks. So to establish his anti-DC bona fides, he boasted that he "shuns the Washington cocktail circuit and backroom card games to spend time romping with his nine children and teaching Sunday school."

What a sanctimonious drip, I was thinking as I approached Anderson for a quick post-lecture interview and photograph. By way of breaking the ice I mentioned that an uncle of mine, Jack Morris, was a long-time editor at the Washington bureau of *The New York Times*, and I wondered if they might have crossed paths. Anderson waved the suggestion away, muttering something about not fraternizing with the rest of the Washington press. Oh right, I thought, you don't spend your spare times at cocktail parties or card games, because you're busy romping with your nine kids and teaching Sunday school. Jack Anderson taught me something else worth knowing: that self-importance can try to dress itself in the weeds of humility, but it will always shine through.

My other story that day was a front-page double byline with Brad, date-lined "Ellenville, New York," about the murder of another local teenage girl. The battered body of Deborah S. Caruso, who'd spent the past eight years in Chambersburg, had been found in a park on Long Island. She had not been sexually assaulted. No psychic had come in to help solve the case. Compared to Debbie Sue Kline, this poor girl's death was almost routine. The story had a short shelf life, and then we moved on.

BUT JUST BECAUSE A REPORTER has no interest in important people doesn't give him the luxury of ignoring a specimen when one wanders into his crosshairs.

So I got busy when I got a tip from a disgruntled teacher about a potentially juicy story shortly after the Debbie Sue Kline and Deborah S. Caruso nightmares faded from the front page.

In the small world of my schools beat, Dr. Robert Kochenour qualified as very big game. He was super-intendent of the Chambersburg Area School District, a fiefdom that sprawled across 250 square miles of Franklin County, and I thought of him as a discount Dick Nixon—same swarthy bluish jowls, same imperious attitude, same loathing for the news media. I despised the guy, and it was apparent the feeling was mutual.

According to my source, Kochenour was sitting on an unpleasant bit of news. In 1975, eleventh graders at Chambersburg Area Senior High School had scored significantly lower in all seven categories of the standardized Iowa Tests of Educational Development, compared with a decade earlier. In 1966, local students had been above the national average in all seven categories; now they were below the national average in three.

Kochenour refused to confirm the story or release the test results. Brad, with his unerring nose for a good story, jumped at the chance to work this one with me. It wasn't exactly Watergate, but it would have to do. We pressured Kochenour until, finally, he called a carefully staged press conference to release the test results with his spin doctor, Wilmot Gabler, the director of Pupil Personnel Services, on hand to explain why the test results were no cause for alarm. Chambersburg's students weren't declining, Gabler claimed with a straight face, the rest of the country's were rising.

Brad and I became obsessed with the story, and we beat on it every day, trying to keep the pot boiling. We questioned whether the school board's closed "work sessions" were a violation of the state's new Sunshine Law. We talked to teachers and students about the lack of curriculum coordination, about their theories on why the scores had declined. In an inspired touch, we broke the story that seven administrators and school board members were attending a convention in Las Vegas, at taxpayer expense, that offered "lessons in the ancient art of belly dancing" and "a special presentation on the life of a Las Vegas showgirl." In Franklin County, that qualified as juicy, if not scandalous, news. On the day we broke that story, coincidentally, Merle Unger tried to escape from the Maryland Penitentiary using a hacksaw blade, but he was recaptured in a crawl space on the roof of the cellblock and returned to his cell.

I recall Katy Hamilton viewing our feverish efforts on the Kochenour story with a cocked eyebrow. As city editor, it was her job to be skeptical when her young reporters came to her panting about our latest earth-shattering scoop, something we did on a more or less daily basis. Her skepticism seemed to rise a notch when it became apparent Brad and I were not merely writing about test scores, we were trying to knock down a pillar of the community, a highly educated educator (what H. L. Mencken derided as an "educationist"), the owner of a master's and a doctorate from Columbia University. Katy had to weigh tricky questions. Was it true, as Brad and I were trying to show, that the decline in test scores meant the entire school system was in decline—and that the blame should be laid at Kochenour's door? Or, as Kochenour and his minions were trying to contend, was the decline in test scores a minor matter, an inevitable result of trends at work throughout contemporary society? In the end, it was impossible for us to establish a direct cause-and-effect link. The hoped-for uproar among readers failed to materialize, possibly because no one wants to be told his kid is dumb and getting dumber. Our earth-shattering scoops turned out to be a mere blip in Kochenour's long career.

Though our stories failed to dislodge Kochenour, they confirmed an uneasy suspicion that had been growing inside me. It seemed almost like a dirty secret, given the mission we were on and the post-Watergate era we were living in, and I didn't want to admit it to Brad or anyone else at the paper. It was this: I had no interest in imparting cold information, or in uncovering and exposing dark acts, or in bagging "big" game like Kochenour. My heart simply wasn't in it. I was faking it. What interested me was both much simpler and much more profound: I wanted to get the ninth guy on the bench to open up to me, then I wanted to tell his story. For Brad, newspaper writing was an end in itself; for me, it would never be more than a means to my chosen end. I kept my secret to myself.

Death by Chaw

Like doctors and cops, reporters tend to cultivate a black sense of humor to help them cope with the things they see every day. This was especially true when it came to covering crime stories. Police reports are oxygen to small-town newspapers—and to more than a few big-city papers—and so this routine duty was taken seriously. It entailed visiting the borough police head-quarters downtown and the state police barracks off US 11 south of town every day, flipping through the reports and picking out the tasty morsels, including all violent crimes and deaths.

One winter morning the regular cop reporter was out sick, and I got tabbed to fill in. At the state police bar-racks, I picked up a fatal: a local man had died when his snowmobile collided head-on with another snow-mobile. I asked the desk sergeant if he could give me any details, and he told me that the two snowmobilers, a thirty-four-year-old man and a sixteen-year-old girl, were out bombing around on a farmer's field about six miles south of town. They were both speeding up oppo-site sides of a swale, straight toward each other, neither rider apparently able to see the approaching snowmo-bile or hear it over the engine's roar. They reached the crest at the same instant, and the machines smashed together, head-on. Both snowmobiles began to burn.

The man, Raymond E. Poe, was pronounced dead on arrival at Chambersburg Hospital. It was the cause of death that caught my eye: asphyxiation. I asked the cop how it was possible to die of asphyxiation after a snowmobile crash in the middle of a cornfield.

I can remember him giving me a twisted smile—cops, as I say, have their own dark sense of humor—and then telling me I would have to get that from the coroner. But I couldn't get the coroner on the phone before the noon deadline, so my front-page story was just four work-manlike paragraphs that didn't even merit a by-line.

Eventually, I reached the coroner, and the next day I wrote a follow-up that was even shorter than the original story, but much juicier. When I asked the coroner, Dr. John P. Manges, the same question I'd asked the cop, he replied, "He choked to death on a cut of tobacco."

Of all the embarrassing, dumbass, hick ways to die, I thought, smashing into another snowmobile and having a plug of tobacco lodge in your windpipe had to be right up there with chasing a deer, tripping, and blowing your own brains out.

As I started typing my follow-up, I kept thinking that it was a shame the just-the-facts-ma'am format of the police report left no room for the life lessons such inane deaths were trying to teach us. Possible headlines ran through my mind as I typed: *Red Man claims local man . . . Don't chew and drive . . .*

The headline that made it into the paper was almost aggressively unimaginative. It read: *Snowmobile victim 'choked to death.'* I still haven't figured out why the headline writer inserted those quotation marks. There was no reason to qualify anything. Raymond E. Poe, pure and simple, choked to death on chaw.

Desperate Living

Though Chambersburg felt like it was sealed inside a bubble deep in the middle of nowhere, it was actually within shouting distance of a number of tantalizing attractions. Baltimore, Washington, Philadelphia, Pittsburgh, even New York City could all be reached within a few hours.

Most American cities were a mess in those days—dirty, dangerous, wobbling on the lip of financial ruin. A few years earlier, President Ford had told New York City to drop dead, and it had nearly obliged. Baltimore might have been in even worse shape, the crime rate off the charts, racial tension at a constant boil. This was before Camden Yards and the spruced-up inner harbor papered over the reality that great swaths of the city were, and still are, Dickensian wastelands, where drug dealers and other career criminals openly work their trades. The myth of a reborn city, promoted most vigorously by crime-fighting Mayor Martin O'Malley, managed to persist despite the true-crime books of David Simon, the popular TV series *The Wire,* and some devastating investigative journalism in *The Baltimore Sun,* much of it written by my talented friend Jim Haner. The myth was finally punctured in 2015, when fed-up citizens rioted after a handcuffed black man, Freddie Gray, died while in police custody. At last people looked under the wallpaper to discover that the wall had been spider-webbed with cracks all along.

But getting away from Chambersburg from time to time was vital to our sanity, so when Maude told me her father was an artist who taught at Maryland Institute, we didn't hesitate. We headed for Baltimore.

Tom Scott turned out to be a warm, gregarious man without a hint of artsy pretension about him. He lived in an art-stuffed row house on West Mount Royal Avenue with his girlfriend Diana, a psychiatrist who was considerably more imposing than affable Tom. Like most Baltimore row houses, theirs had a backyard that ended at an alley that ran the length of the block. As we sat in the backyard on warm evenings drinking beer and talking, it was not uncommon to hear the *whap whap whap* of shoe leather as someone sprinted down the darkened alley. This was usually followed by the roar of the police department's helicopter swooping toward us, its spotlight stroking the alley and back yards and rooftops, trying to locate the sprinting suspect and frequently bathing us in hot, white light. The helicopter was known as Fox Trot, and its roar rendered conversation impossible, so we learned to sit there, mute and phosphorescent, until the thing zooped away. Baltimore was strictly Fritz the Cat, sharp movements out of the corner of the eye, Big Brother chasing lots of bad, bad guys. We knew we weren't in Chambersburg anymore, which was, of course, the whole point.

One night Tom decided to give us a dose of local color. He got tickets to an advance screening of *Desperate Living,* the latest trash and gore fest from Baltimore's beloved native son, John Waters. The director and his leading "lady" from earlier pictures, Divine, were in the house that night. Tom and Maude and I sat in the back row, behind an enormous black woman who was sitting next to a chiseled slab of a guy who looked like he might have been a professional boxer. The crowd was keyed up, hoping for something thoroughly disgusting.

The lights went down, and the movie opened with a rich, white doctor squabbling with his crazy wife. She brains him with a bottle and screams for her maid. Grizelda Brown, an enormous black woman, answers the summons and promptly sits on the dazed doctor, killing him. This drew shrieks of delight from the crowd. Then the two confederates flee the murder scene, only to start squabbling among themselves. The furious Grizelda drags the white woman out of the car and tells her, "I ain't your maid anymore, bitch. I'm your sister in crime!"

As the room convulsed, I noticed that the woman sitting in front of us was gleefully pounding the boxer's arm. Those rabbit punches had to hurt, but the man took his punishment without flinching. That was when I realized the puncher was Jean Hill, the actress playing Grizelda Brown up on the screen. I was having my view of the movie blocked by three hundred-pounds worth of Baltimore royalty! We weren't merely watching a John Waters movie. We were *in* one.

On another trip, Tom agreed to accompany us on the obligatory tour of The Block, Baltimore's notorious "adult entertainment" zone, a DMZ that was, miraculously, even sleazier than New York's Times Square. It was a high-noon neon world of game rooms, show bars, touts, XXX peep shows, and strippers with names like Lola and Blaze Starrr.

We settled on a grim, little strip joint. I don't remember the name of the dive, but I do recall that it had the yeasty smell of a frat house toilet early on a Sunday morning, and the dancers worked on a tongue-shaped stage behind the horseshoe bar. When serving customers, the lucky bartender had his back turned to the stage.

None of it was pretty—not the watery, overpriced drinks, not the dancers, and certainly not the things the dancers were doing. The most memorable performer was a white woman with Russ Meyer breasts and some impressive cottage-cheese cellulite who was so drunk she could barely stand up, let alone dance. Wisely, she decided to get down on the stage floor for some serious grinding, only to discover that she was unable to stand back up. So she just kept writhing on the floor. Eventually, the word *protoplasm* came to me.

After this had gone on a little too long, Tom turned to us with a delighted smile and said, "Gives a whole new meaning to the concept of a floor show, doesn't it?"

Indeed it did. And I had come to understand, at last, why they call Baltimore "Charm City."

Talent Pool

Such weekend getaways were salutary but too rare. Work kept getting in the way. Many workdays stretched from dawn till midnight, and then, for good measure, I frequently spent weekends interviewing people for feature stories. There wasn't much time for road trips to catch the latest John Waters movie or a floor show on The Block.

Everyone on the *Public Opinion* staff lived monastic lives that had little room for anything other than work. David Scott Smith probably put in the longest hours, thanks to those ever-murmuring police scanners. And yet David, like the rest of us, was not inclined to complain. The simple reason was that we loved what we were doing, and we were all young enough and passionate enough and naïve enough to look past the fact that we were being shamelessly exploited. This was the evil genius of the Gannett empire.

I once asked David to single out the worst thing about his job, assuming it would be getting rousted from sleep to photograph dead-of-night fires and car wrecks, or possibly getting forced to make those ludicrous portraits of deer hunters and their inert trophies. But he surprised me. "I *liked* doing my job," he said, "and I had a lot of respect for the cops and firefighters. The thing that bothered me most was grab-and-grins."

This is newspaper shorthand for the most un-photogenic ritual known to mankind—one group of beaming officials handing a check to another group of beaming officials, such as the time David immortalized a "vector control specialist" from the state Department of Environmental Control passing a $4,000 check to three Franklin County commissioners. (A vector, according to my dictionary, is "an organism, such as a mosquito or a tick, that carries disease-causing micro-organisms from one host to another.") "This happened every night," David added, "after you'd started working at 7:30 in the morning. I kept asking myself, *This is why I went to journalism school?*"

It wasn't until many years later that I came to understand that another of *Public Opinion*'s more prosaic staples—those ubiquitous pictures of car crashes—could be the stuff of high art. This understanding began to take shape on a spring day in 2003 when I walked into a New York art gallery and found the walls lined with curious black-and-white photographs of cars and trucks in the contorted aftermaths of various mishaps: a Mercedes impaled by a phone pole, a crunched Simca teetering on a bridge guard rail, a Citroen with a mangled snout, a VW resting on its roof in a shallow river, even a motorboat beached in the middle of a rain-slickened roadway. The mountainous background scenery was often postcard pretty. The pictures were expertly composed and lit. There were no people in them. These pictures were the unadorned, nearly clinical documentation of mechanized disasters. And yet there was no doubt they were works of art.

Looking at them, I recalled the pictures that appeared nearly every day on the front page of *Public Opinion*—a Ford Pinto's passenger door crushed by a phone pole, the crumpled grille of an Oldsmobile, a VW resting on its side as firefighters work to free the driver, who had fallen asleep at the wheel and woke up pinned beneath his car.

That flashback in the New York art gallery might have been the moment when the idea for this book germinated, the moment when I began to believe that my life in Chambersburg was worth revisiting. The photographer who took those pictures in the New York art gallery was named Arnold Odermatt. He worked as a traffic policeman in the Swiss canton of Nidwalden from 1948 to 1990, and one of his duties was to document motor vehicle accidents for insurance companies and police reports. He frequently took another set of pictures for himself, the unpeopled pictures on the gallery wall, strangely quiet and peaceful, sometimes humorous, far removed from the sounds of shrieking rubber and exploding glass that produced these eerily serene pictures.

At about the time I was discovering Odermatt's photographs, the British writer Geoff Dyer was publishing an essay about a very different chronicler of automotive mayhem, the Mexican photographer Enrique Metinides. Unlike Odermatt, Metinides photographed the crowds of gawkers who gathered around the twisted wrecks on the streets of Mexico City, like pilgrims drawn to a holy site. Looking at a picture by Metinides becomes a complex transaction: we look not only at the evidence of a disaster, but also at the people who have come to bear witness, and we look at them looking at us. Dyer cites Cormac McCarthy's conviction that "nothing can be proven except that it be made to bleed. Virgins, bulls, men. Ultimately God himself." As countries like Mexico remind us, the more fervent the religious beliefs, the bloodier the religious icons.

"This," Dyer writes, "is why faces of the people in Metinides' photographs have a look of shock or astonishment but never of disbelief. His photographs, in fact, are of *believers.* The catastrophes visited upon them actually confirm people in their belief in the bloody way things are, have been, and always will be."

Odermatt and Metinides led me to new discoveries and associations. The German publisher Taschen, maker of the artsiest of art books, produced *Car Crashes & Other Sad Stories,* a showcase of the work of Mel Kilpatrick, who worked as a news photographer in southern California in the 1940s and '50s, chronicling the deadly effects of the region's burgeoning post-war car culture. Here, in addition to the twisted metal and the people who have come to bear witness, we get bloody, mutilated corpses. The horror moves some bystanders to laughter, a reaction that seems appalling at first, but then strangely apposite. For isn't laughter the spontaneous admission that our expectations have been upended, and we have no other way to cope with the ambush? Isn't laughter a reflexive response to fear?

Meanwhile, an amateur photographer named Irwin Norling was amassing a chronicle of a very different post-war boomtown, the Minneapolis suburb of Bloomington. Norling photographed the gamut of suburban life, including parades, weddings, town council meetings, baseball games, shopping center parking lots, Levittown-ish housing developments and, of course, car crashes. In *Suburban World: The Norling Photos,* published in 2008, Brad Zellar writes, "Norling's pictures provide both a sort of suburban taxonomy as well as a civics lesson in black and white, complete with a thorough exploration of the dark undertow that runs beneath even the sleepiest little towns."

This strikes me as a marvelous summation of what we did every day at *Public Opinion.* But our taxonomy had strict ground rules. While the pictures of Metinides and Kilpatrick (and the car crash paintings of Andy

Warhol in his *Death and Disaster* series) clearly succeed as records of spectacles and as spectacles in their own right, the car crash pictures of Odermatt, Norling, and the *Public Opinion* staff succeeded at a far more delicate and vital task: they were reassuring. This, I believe, begins to explain why the readers of *Public Opinion* had an insatiable appetite for pictures of wrecks, fires, and other mayhem. They found these pictures reassuring on several levels. First, and most obvious, anyone holding a newspaper and looking at a picture of a smashed car will feel relief that he wasn't inside that car. There is a related forensic aspect to this relief, especially in a small town—the newspaper reader checking to see if he knows the identity of any of the victims, a likelihood that rises as the size of the town shrinks.

This level of relief may be obvious, but it quickly deepens. The picture is also reassuring because it is a portrait of an aberration, a rare and fleeting instant when the smooth fabric of everyday life is torn. The presence of firefighters and ambulance crews in the picture promises that the tear is temporary and order will soon be restored. This, in turn, provides perhaps the most profound relief of all for residents of a Swiss canton like Nidwalden or a small American town like Chambersburg: everyday life in such a place might be predictable, even a grinding bore at times, but shocking drama *does* happen.

PHOTOGRAPHERS AREN'T THE ONLY PEOPLE who turn such small dramas into art. Walker Percy's first novel, *The Moviegoer*, is built around one man's campaign to overcome the everydayness of everyday life. His name is Binx Bolling. He's a milquetoasty stockbroker who lives in a bland New Orleans suburb, where he's involved in an idiosyncratic quest he calls "the search." Binx says:

What is the nature of the search? you ask.

Really it is very simple, at least for a fellow like me; so simple that it is easily overlooked.

The search is what everyone would undertake if he was not sunk in the everydayness of his own life. . . . To become aware of the possibility of the search is to be onto something. Not to be onto something is to be in despair.

Despair, which Binx also calls "the malaise," comes from being so sunk in the everyday that you don't even realize you're sunk. Binx experiences minor escapes from everydayness, little epiphanies, such as when he pauses to consider the contents of his own pockets—wallet, keys, handkerchief, pencil:

What was unfamiliar about them was that I could see them. They might have belonged to someone else. A man can look at this little pile on his bureau for thirty years and never once see it. It is as invisible as his own hand.

Finally, Binx is sprung from this killing everydayness by a much bigger epiphany: a car crash. He's out for a drive with his secretary:

Early afternoon finds us spinning along the Gulf Coast. Things have not gone too badly. As luck would have it, no sooner do we cross Bay St. Louis and reach the beach drive than we are involved in an accident. Fortunately it is not serious. When I say as luck would have it, I mean good luck. Yet how, you might wonder, can even a minor accident be considered good luck?

Because it provides a means of winning out over the malaise, if one has the sense to take advantage of it.

Though they probably couldn't have put it into words, I'm convinced the readers of *Public Opinion* felt this same shiver of good luck every time they saw a picture of a car crash in the paper, and possibly even when, like Binx, they were involved in a minor accident. The everyday is, briefly, vanquished. We are, briefly, alive in the moment. Everything is astonishing, strange, new. A car resting on its roof! An airplane in a tree! To make sure the shock remained reassuring, *Public Opinion* had a strict policy of never showing the bodies of accident victims.

The absence of dead or damaged bodies in Arnold Odermatt's pictures sprang from a motive far loftier than discretion. He wanted to operate above the level of lurid sensationalism (à la Warhol or Weegee), in a place where he was free to make pure portraits of the surprisingly beautiful and balletic consequences of mechanical failure, human error, or simple bad luck. That's why Odermatt's pictures rise to the level of art. Like Walker Percy pausing to notice the contents of his pockets on the bureau, Odermatt reminds us that art is not about knowing what to look at; it's about knowing how to notice, and how to see.

REPORTERS WERE EXPECTED to be on the constant lookout for fires, wrecks, fallen trees, downed power lines, any ripple on the surface of the everyday that might be turned into a photo or a story or both. I didn't own a camera, so I usually borrowed one from David when I went off on a feature story, and yet I can't recall ever taking a picture of a fire or a car wreck. With that lone exception, I was, like everyone else on the staff, always on duty.

We may have been united by our galley-slave work ethic, but I came to realize there were two distinct types pulling the oars in that newsroom. There were those who were delighted to be living and working in a small town in central nowhere (the stay-heres); and there were those who couldn't wait to get away (the outta-heres).

Generally, though not always, your affiliation was determined by your place of origin.

Jean Covert, for instance, had all the makings of a
Public Opinion lifer. She was from tiny Orbisonia, not
far from Shade Gap, where the Mountain Man had run
his terror campaign back in the 1960s. After earning
a degree in sociology from nearby Shippensburg State
College, Jean got hired at *Public Opinion* in 1974, and
she was active in the Fayetteville Volunteer Fire Department, just east of Chambersburg. She was a hard
worker and a solid reporter, with a twinkle of the flirt
about her—the bobbed hair, the snug sweaters, the
short skirts. Jeanie, as we called her, was frozen in time
and place. Her time was the pre-hippie '60s, and small-
town Pennsylvania was her place. She often joked that
she was "a hick from the sticks" who'd made it all the
way to the "big city." But you got the idea that the joke
was no joke, that Chambersburg was plenty big enough
for Jean Covert.

But all stay-heres weren't born locally, and all trans-
plants weren't necessarily outta-heres. Marie Lanser, a
peripatetic Army brat in her youth, wound up settling
in the area. Katy Hamilton, the city editor, was born
on a farm in the state of Pomerania, near Germany's
Baltic coast. As the Russians advanced at the end of
the Second World War, her family fled toward Finland,
only to get intercepted by Russian troops and sent back
home. They returned to discover that their farmhouse
had been burned to the ground. After surviving the horrors of a displaced-persons camp, Katy went to work
as a teletype operator at the Frankfurt Airport in the
1950s, where she met and married an American ser-
viceman named Robert Hamilton, who was from Chambersburg. Eventually, they moved to his hometown, and
in 1960, three weeks after giving birth to her second
daughter, Katy went to work as a teletype operator at

Public Opinion for $1 an hour, beginning her long climb to the managing editor's chair. When *The Philadelphia Bulletin* sent out job feelers, Katy rebuffed them. She knew all about being uprooted, and she was determined to give her daughters a stable home. She may have been born an ocean away, but Katy, like Jean Covert, had the makings of a Chambersburg lifer.

So did the paper's obituary writer, Harriet Rhodes, who looked like she needed to get busy writing her own obituary. Harriet was beyond prelapsarian; she was prehistoric. As far as anyone knew, she'd been working at the paper since its founding in 1869. She had big, rheumy eyes that made her look like an anime character made of melting wax. Everyone adored her. She could remember the days when the paper routinely covered funerals of prominent citizens as news events, and there was a hat and a pair of white gloves in the newsroom for Harriet to wear whenever she got sent out to immortalize the departed. One day, after taking a call from a funeral director, she slammed down her receiver and began cackling gleefully. We all looked at her. When she got hold of herself, she cried, "How in the world is it possible for a ninety-eight-year-old woman to die *unexpectedly*?!"

Then there were the misfits like myself and my roommate. Brad Bumsted was pure Pennsylvanian. He was born and raised in York, just fifty miles from Chambersburg, and he got a degree in history from Indiana University of Pennsylvania, but he loathed everything about Franklin County. He referred to the place as "Happy Valley," a baldly ironic poaching of the honorific Penn State University loyalists had bestowed on State College, where the head coach of the Nittany Lions football team, Joe Paterno, was revered as a deity, and where one of his assistants, Jerry Sandusky, had just opened a charity for under-privileged youths called The

Second Mile. David Scott Smith was born and raised in suburban Washington, DC, and his kinetic energy and obvious talent made it unlikely that he would stick around long. Dawn DeCwikiel-Kane, from suburban Philadelphia, looked like another short-timer.

It was David who made the first move. When he was studying journalism at Ohio University, one of his professors had put him in touch with a Gannett talent scout, who was so impressed by David's pictures that he started circulating them to Gannett editors. "Congratulations," David's professor told him, "you're now an official member of the Gannett talent pool." He neglected to add, "Be careful what you wish for."

That contact led to an interview with Bob Collins and a job offer at *Public Opinion* shortly after David's graduation in the summer of 1974. When Collins hired David, he told him to expect to work hard. "If you can make it here," Collins said, "every place else you work will be like summer camp."

Now, after three years of boot camp, David was ready for a taste of summer camp. Since he was already swimming in the Gannett talent pool, he started sending his portfolio to other Gannett papers in smallish cities that were a step up from Chambersburg: Ft. Myers, Florida; Olympia, Washington; and San Bernardino, California. No job offers ensued. Though David didn't know it at the time, several of the editors who'd received his portfolio wanted to offer him a job, but when they called Collins for a reference, he told them he didn't want to lose David. So in keeping with corporate etiquette, the editors looked elsewhere. Talent, it turned out, could actually be an impediment to getting off this galley.

We outta-heres, unaware of these behind-the-scenes machinations, kept our heads down and pulled hard on our oars. But we always kept one eye fixed on the exit sign.

Hers Is a Lush Situation

When that brutal winter finally loosened its grip, I decided it was time to take advantage of one of my job's few perks. In addition to all those mind-fogging school board meetings, my beat included the Franklin County Area Vocational Technical School, known as the Vo-Tech. There lay opportunity.

I loved the place—the shops, the tools, the gearhead instructors teaching kids to work with their hands, to make things and fix things instead of buying things and throwing them out and then buying more. The practical nature of the place appealed to me on several levels. It had been drummed into my head from an early age that I would be going to college. My father's father had been a professor for more than half a century, and my father had graduated from college and had always done white-collar work, first as a newspaper reporter, then in the PR hive at the Ford Motor Company. I don't believe the man ever got his hands dirty or broke a sweat. In high school, like father like son, I concentrated on history and literature, not circular saws and socket wrenches. It was only after I dropped out of college and traveled the country that I began to appreciate the satisfactions of manual labor, of building things, tinkering with my car, fixing stuff.

On another level, I loved the Vo-Tech because it was built on the highly un-American notion that not every student is college material, *and that's not a bad thing.* I never bought into the ideas that a college degree is a badge of intelligence or that "shop class" is for dummies and losers. We will always need qualified plumbers and electricians and welders. And as history has shown, they enjoy far greater job security than newspaper reporters.

One day a teacher in the Vo-Tech auto body shop remarked on the rust spots freckling the dark-green skin of my '54 Buick, and he told me his students would love to get their hands on such a classic. If I bought the sandpaper, Bond-O and paint, the labor would be free. Figuring my $140 weekly paycheck entitled me to such a perk, I jumped at the offer, settling on a two-tone color scheme: hot pink for the car's midriff, with black on the roof and black below the chrome sweepspears that swooped along the car's flanks. The car was built the year Elvis cut his first records, so I guess I was thinking this was a paintjob worthy of the King.

While digging in some files recently searching for my birth certificate, I noticed a piece of paper peeking out of a folder. Along the edge of this paper, in bright red letters, were the words ALL WORK DONE BY STUDENTS ON AN EXPERIMENTAL LEARNING BASIS. Intrigued, I pulled the paper out of the file and was stunned to discover that it was the receipt from my Vo-Tech paintjob, dated April 19, 1977. I had no idea I'd been dragging this document around for nearly four decades. Once again, a piece of my past had found me at the precise moment I needed it.

The bill spelled out that the parts—"sheet metal, body plastic, primer, sandpaper, masking tape, 5 qts. Acrylic enamel paint"—cost me $82.25. The receipt was signed by "R. Kalb," with the notation "Paid, 6- ." I assume the incomplete date of the payment meant I picked the

car up sometime in June, which meant it must have spent a couple of months in the shop. Students at the Vo-Tech didn't do rush jobs. With tax my total bill came to just $87.19. Not even Earl Scheib painted a car for so little.

Some two decades after my Buick got Elvisized in the Vo-Tech auto body shop, I published an essay called "Hers Is a Lush Situation," in which I tried to explain how that car became my Muse. The essay began:

> It was love at first sight – not because she was perfect, but because she was so lush with possibility. The object of a man's love is like that, always possessing highly specific virtues while emitting a sense of what she has a chance to become.
>
> In this case she possessed curves that were ample, sometimes breathtaking, but never vulgar. She sparkled. She turned heads. She looked like she was in motion even when she was standing still; and when moved, she flew. Her skin was bad in spots, a terrible dark color. But as I say, she was not about perfection, she was about possibility.
>
> And the price was right. I picked her up for $250.

Even then, during Nixon's second term, that was a steal for a 1954 Buick Century in good running condition. Yes, the upholstery was frayed, the starter sometimes balky, and there were rust spots sprouting on her atrocious midnight-green paintjob. Yet her charms were undeniable. Her bulging contours, lavish slabs of chrome, and three fender notches left no doubt that she was from an earlier era – a time, as John Cheever put it, when New York City was still filled with a river light and almost everybody wore a hat. It was different from the time when I bought the car, 1974, when Americans were getting used to oil embargoes and disco and the notion that their president was a crook and Detroit was sinking into its deepest stylistic Sargasso. I think of the seventies and I think of Ricardo Montalban purring about the "rich Corinthian leather" inside that bloodless box, the Chrysler Cordoba.

My essay went on to explain that after I got the car painted, I began to study the history of its design, especially the "wraparound windshield," a major styling and engineering innovation—and selling point—in General Motors' 1954 lineup. The "panoramic" windshield, according to *Industrial Design* magazine, did not improve the driver's vision (which I already knew), but it "did more than any other single development to make last year's models out of date overnight."

In other words, form had become more important than function. Appearance was now all. With that realization, my car became more than a car. My essay continued:

My Buick had begun to reveal its true purpose. It was giving me a way to write about the world that made us. I already knew that America in 1954 was flush with victory, eager for the seductive flash of consumer goods, poised for blastoff. The more I learned about that pivotal year, though, the less

it had to do with the stereotype of bland Eisenhower conformity. Rather, I came to see it as a year of bubbling ferment
– artistic, political, social, sexual, racial. It was a year that
had room not only for the wraparound windshield and the
H-bomb, but for everything in between – the first recordings
of Elvis Presley, the final defeat of the French in Vietnam,
the beginning of the end of school segregation, the censure
of Joe McCarthy, the marriage and divorce of Joe DiMaggio
and Marilyn Monroe, and the appearance of color television
and McDonald's golden arches. Nabokov was finishing *Lo-
lita* and Kerouac was finishing *On the Road*. This rich frenzy
formed the backdrop for what would become my first novel.

But before that novel got written, before my Buick
even made it out of the Vo-Tech auto body shop, Brad
dropped a bombshell. He had agreed to take a job with
the Gannett-owned *Valley News Dispatch,* a dozen
miles upriver from Pittsburgh. He would be the paper's
reporter in Pittsburgh, covering the Allegheny County
Courthouse and the rest of the city. It was a huge step
up from Chambersburg.

We had a big send-off in our apartment. In keeping
with the "lame duck" theme of the evening, someone
produced a large, plastic goose, which actually started
to look a bit like a duck after the Labatt's beers went
to work. Someone else brought a bunch of tapes, so
we weren't limited to our regular diet of Al Green and
Rufus, and our living room turned into a sweaty dance
floor as the evening lifted off. Everyone was there, the
Public Opinion staff, reporters from other papers, lawyers and government officials, and they were all coming
together to say farewell to a reporter who was liked by
most and respected by all.

One of the more thoughtful guests gave Brad a going-
away present to keep him warm on lonely Pittsburgh
nights—an inflatable love doll, her mouth frozen in a

circular Edvard Munch fellatio-ready scream. It was love at first sight for Brad and the doll, and he spent the rest of the night making eyes at his new love interest, to the delight of our guests.

When things started getting ragged well past midnight, someone had the brilliant idea that it was time for the lame duck to die. We all piled outside onto the sidewalk to watch the plastic goose take a human-assisted stroll across South Second Street, just as the light at the corner turned green. The first dragster to leap from the starting line was a red Corvette, which ran over the skidding goose, a horrible crunching noise. The driver of the Corvette stomped on his brakes and sprang from the car. The poor goose had been slaughtered, hundreds of shards of plastic strewn across the pavement. Cars stopped behind the Corvette, horns blared. We had brought the Peanut Circuit to a standstill.

Seeing the crowd on the sidewalk, the owner of the Corvette came at us, his blood up. "Who threw that fucking goose under my car?" he demanded.

"That wasn't a goose," someone said, "it was a duck." We all roared. Someone else explained that it ran out of the building before anyone could stop it. More laughter. A lawyer handed the outraged driver a business card and said he would be willing to provide legal representation if the man got sued by PETA or the ASPCA for animal cruelty. Tom Kelchner produced a pen and a reporter's notebook and started to interview the driver, asking in a deadpan voice if the duck was running or flying at the moment of impact. As our merriment grew, the anger leaked out of the guy, and he went back to his car, shaking his head, muttering. As he drove off into the night, tires squealing, our delight accelerated with the car.

The next day Brad left for Pittsburgh, and I found myself living alone again. This time I was in an empty three-story apartment with a toilet bowl and dozens of empty beer bottles in the living room and a love doll on the kitchen floor. All the air had leaked out of her, but her red lips were still frozen in a perfect O.

A Death in the Family

Bam bam bam bam! Bam bam bam bam BAM!

My eyes opened, and I was looking at the ceiling of my third-story bedroom, the attic I'd moved into after Brad left for Pittsburgh. What was that noise?

Bam bam bam bam bam bam BAM!

The light in the room was milky blue, the sun not yet up. Someone was banging on the front door of my apartment.

I went to the window and stuck my head out. Down on the sidewalk a uniformed cop was raising his fist to bang again on my door. "Can I help you?" I called down to him.

He looked up, took a moment to locate the head sticking out of the window. "Are you Bill Morris?"

What did I do wrong? Should I lie? It was too early to puzzle it out. I said, "Yessir."

"Your father's going to call you at the newspaper office at seven o'clock. He says it's important."

The realization came to me, so swift and sudden it was irrefutable, an iron fact: *My mother's dead.*

Since my Buick was still at the Vo-Tech, I walked to the paper as early sunshine poured through the trees. The day was going to be hot. I tried to talk myself out of the realization that had hit me as I'd looked down at the cop, but it was no use. I felt like I was being led to the gallows.

There were only a few early birds in the office when I arrived. I sat down and stared at my phone, praying it would not ring, that there had been some mistake, that this was a bad dream. The phone rang a few minutes after seven.

I heard my father say, "Your mother's dead, Son."

"I had a feeling. What happened?"

He told me a disjointed story about my brother Rick returning home from school early that morning. Rick had put his wild hippie days behind him and enrolled in Syracuse University's architecture school, where students frequently pulled all-nighters. To save money, he was living in the basement bedroom in our parents' house. When Rick got home around 3:30 that morning, my father went on, he saw a light upstairs and went up to check on our mother. Our father was in New York City on a business trip. Rick found our mother sprawled on her bathroom floor, dressed in pajamas. There was a trickle of vomit. She was already dead.

"Do they know the cause of death?" I asked.

"They think it was a heart attack."

I told my father I was on my way and would be home in five hours or so. Maude loaned me her back-up car, a rickety, mustard-yellow Fiat, and I got on I-81 and headed north.

MY FATHER AND BROTHER had already returned from making arrangements at the funeral home by the time my two sisters and I arrived in Syracuse. The casket was going to be closed. I had seen the last of my mother.

We were like sleepwalkers, my father and my siblings and I, going through unfamiliar motions on some sort of mysterious Jungian auto-pilot. We were all too shocked to be shocked. Our mother had been two weeks shy of her fifty-seventh birthday, apparently in good health, a survivor of cancer with no history of heart disease. This wasn't happening.

I tried to get my brother to go into more detail about his grim discovery that morning. He's the eldest, and he has always been remote, loath to share his feelings, and he simply locked me out, said he wasn't ready to talk about it yet.

Next I went at my father. On the phone that morning he'd said they *think* it was a heart attack. Surely there was going to be an autopsy?

"What good will an autopsy do?" my father said. "She'll still be dead."

"Yes," I countered, "but at least we'll know for sure *why* she died." This was the newspaperman in me talking, the young man who wasn't afraid of the truth, wasn't afraid of finding out that my mother's death had been caused by something darker than a faulty heart—an accidental overdose, maybe, or even suicide. My father had been battling alcoholism—rehab, AA, relapse, rehab, AA, relapse, the whole dreary drill—and I'd often suspected that my mother might have had a drinking problem of her own, less obvious than my father's but therefore even more insidious. Maybe she'd had a drunken fall and hit her head. Maybe she'd aspirated her own vomit and choked to death. Maybe she'd swallowed a fistful of pills. Didn't anyone want to know for sure?

The answer was no. My mother was dead, my brother wasn't talking, and my father didn't even want to know how she died. I had entered a world where everything that was happening was beyond my control. I went to bed that night too angry and frustrated to feel grief.

THE HOUSE FILLED WITH FAMILY and friends the next day, with food and booze and chatter that skirted the thing that had brought us together in this house. If my mother was mentioned at all, it was to tell some funny story on her, or to sing her many virtues. She gave me my love for reading and had been quite a beauty as a young woman, and she packed a brown-bag lunch for each of her four children every morning before marching us off to school. She had been working as a volunteer at a nursing home, work she adored. My brother and sisters and I managed to laugh about her execrable cooking—her beef stew was especially notorious—and I believe that was the first time I'd ever cried while laughing. Looking around the crowded house, I understood why alcohol was invented.

Everyone had too much to drink, especially my mother's baby sister, Aunt Recie, a flashy redhead who lived in Boca Raton, Florida, with her golf-happy husband and their three kids. I'd heard vague stories from my mother that Uncle Chuck and Aunt Recie had been having serious troubles with one of their teenage sons, who was in the habit of getting drunk and wrecking cars. When most of the guests had drifted off, I found myself standing by the fireplace in the living room, alone with Aunt Recie, who was half-masted and obviously in a foul mood. "Kids put their mothers through hell," she said.

I was too stunned to be angry. We weren't the Brady Bunch, but we most certainly had not put our mother through hell. Genuine love flowed between her and all four of her children. I didn't know what to say, so I said, "What are you talking about, Aunt Recie?"

"You're all acting so broken up, but it's all a big act. You didn't love your mother."

For the first and only time in my life, I experienced a white-out. Little white dots began sizzling in my peripheral vision, and they expanded until I was seeing my redheaded aunt through a tunnel of white light. I felt clammy. My weight shifted onto my right foot—better for launching a punch—and I felt my right hand close into a fist. Now all I could see was the left side of my aunt's face, the immaculate porcelain jaw I was about to shatter.

"Brother?"

It was my sister Gretchen's voice, coming from far away. She touched my right elbow, and I could feel the anger drain out of me, felt my fist unclench, watched my field of vision return to normal. "Everything okay?" Gretchen said.

I walked away without a word, grateful that I'd been saved from committing a violent act that would have haunted me for the rest of my life. To this day I'm sure my aunt had no idea what had just happened. Or, more to the point, what had just *not* happened. I haven't spoken to her since.

MY MOTHER'S DEATH LED ME, indirectly, to the discovery of that receipt for the Buick's paintjob at the Vo-Tech. As I said, I stumbled upon the receipt while looking through files trying to locate my birth certificate. The reason I needed to find my birth certificate was because I wanted to get a copy of my mother's certificate of death, and the New York State Department of Health, under law, would release it only to a spouse, child, or parent of the deceased. My birth certificate would establish that I am my mother's son, and I was hoping that her certificate of death would help me unravel the mystery of how she died.

My main interest was the official cause of death. There it was, in the handwriting of the Onondaga County Medical Examiner, Dr. Martin Hilfinger Jr.: "Probable arteriosclerotic heart disease." Nearly forty years after the fact, that word *probable* still jumps at me. In a box marked "Approximate Interval Between Onset & Death," Dr. Hilfinger wrote "Sudden." Margaret Anne Morris died at 3:41 a.m. on June 15, 1977. She was at home, alone. There was no autopsy. The cause of death is, as far as I'm concerned, still unknown.

WE BURIED MY MOTHER in a hilly cemetery next to a Catholic church about two miles from where she died. As I watched her casket go into the ground, I was still too numb for anything to register or resonate. It felt like I was walking on the ocean floor, like I was watching a movie of somebody else's life, some stranger pretending to bury his mother. Out of body comes close to describing how I felt.

Months would pass before the finality of my mother's death would hit me and I would be able to begin to grieve. For now, all I wanted to do was get away from Syracuse and lose myself in work. It was the only way to get through this. The next morning I left for Chambersburg, where the old bull-goose lunacy was getting ready to put on its most spectacular show yet.

PART THREE
Gone

Something Happened

Two weeks after I returned to Chambersburg from my mother's funeral, the Fourth of July weekend arrived on a blast-furnace heat wave. That much I remember. But when I try to recreate that weekend and my role in its horrific events, my memory falters. I was sure I'd spent that Saturday, July 2, interviewing a political novice in Mercersburg. Here, drawn from memory, is my first draft of that day's events:

> Determined not to loll around my stuffy apartment, I arranged to spend that Saturday interviewing a quixotic character named Tim O. Rockwell, a history teacher at Maude's alma mater, Mercersburg Academy. Though he had no political experience, Rockwell hoped to unseat a political institution in the upcoming Democratic primary—seven-term incumbent State Rep. William O. Shuman, whose district stretched across southern Franklin County and into neighboring Fulton County. I was glad to have an excuse to do something—anything—that would take my mind off my mother's death.

A nice story, almost touching, but that's not how it happened. As I learned from a reel of microfilm, my article about Rockwell's announcement appeared in

Public Opinion on Wednesday, July 6, under the head-line "Mercersburg Academy teacher to oppose Shuman." It began:

> Tim O. Rockwell, 38, of Mercersburg, yesterday took an early plunge into the political arena with an announcement he'll run for State Representative William O. Shuman's 90th District seat in the May, 1978 primary on the Democratic ticket.
>
> "The time is ripe," Rockwell said at a press conference at the Mercersburg Inn yesterday. "People need change in leadership."

So I had not traveled to Mercersburg on Saturday for a one-on-one interview with Tim Rockwell, as my memory was telling me. I attended Rockwell's press conference the following Tuesday, July 5, and produced a short, factual article in the next day's paper.

So what was I doing on that Saturday? Based on articles of mine that appeared in upcoming editions of the paper, I might have been interviewing students at a summer woodworking shop, or I might have been inter-viewing the head of the Vo-Tech school. Or I might have just been driving back roads drinking beer, determined to escape my stuffy apartment and thoughts about my mother's death. But I have no memory of that day, so I can't say for sure where I was. I can be reasonably sure I wasn't home, though, because Bob Collins, that sandy-haired terrier, would have sent someone to bang on my door as he scrambled to patch together the crew of *Public Opinion* staffers who spent that Saturday afternoon and evening covering one of the most appalling crimes ever to unfold in that quiet corner of the world. I must have been impossible to reach, because I missed the fireworks. But Collins would see to it that I got deeply involved in their aftermath.

AN EX-MARINE NAMED Gary Lee Rock woke up with a hangover that hot Saturday morning on his living room sofa near Fayetteville, a few miles east of Chambersburg. Rock had enlisted during his senior year at Chambersburg Area Senior High School in 1972, and two weeks after graduation, at the pliable age of seventeen, he found himself at Parris Island, South Carolina, enduring the exquisite hell of Marine Corps boot camp. During four years of active duty he would attain the Corps' highest marksmanship rating, "expert," and the events of that Saturday led many to assume that Gary Lee Rock had been traumatized by combat in Vietnam. He had not. His most dangerous duty in the Marines had been tracking down deserters and returning them to the brig. He had never fired a shot in anger. The closest he got to Vietnam was Hawaii.

Rock was fully dressed when he woke up on his sofa that Saturday morning, still wearing the blue shirt and jeans he'd worn to a cookout in Chambersburg the night before. He got invited to the party by Terry Olson, a buddy since fourth grade, but it turned out to be a bad idea. One of the first people Rock spotted at the party was Ann Chestnut, a college student he'd dated a couple of times, nothing serious yet, but Rock was surprised to see her with another guy. Surprised and "kind of hurt," he would admit later. Turning to the proven remedy for such pain, Rock started pounding beers, finishing off "maybe a six pack or so" before heading out to his '69 Ford pickup. When Terry Olson went out to check on his friend, known to intimates as "Bud" or "Buddy," Olson found Rock sitting in the cab of the truck. He was crying.

ROCK HAD PLANNED to spend that Saturday doing landscaping work around his modest wooden house—four rooms plus an unfinished room upstairs—that he'd bought in 1976 for $22,000. It stood alongside a shed in a grassy clearing on three and a half wooded acres, at the end of a long dirt lane that led in from Black Gap Road. Looming behind the property was hump-shouldered South Mountain.

Rock swallowed a couple of aspirin for breakfast. After listening to some music on his pricey stereo— his lone indulgence besides his collection of guns and ammo—he decided to drive to the bank in Chambersburg. He needed cash because of yesterday's unwelcome surprise. Friday was payday at Letterkenny Army Depot, where Rock had worked the past nine months as a production clerk in a facility that refurbished tanks. It wasn't Rock's first job since his discharge from the Marines the previous summer. He'd gotten on as a welding trainee at Grove Manufacturing but found he hated the work, hated the boss even more, and after a few days he quit. He was turned down for unemployment benefits because he'd walked off the job, and he had to pick apples to make his house payments. At the time, Rock was dating a woman who got a job offer in a distant town. He urged her to turn the job down, but she took it and left him. Money got so tight he even thought about re-upping in the Marines. Finally, in the fall, he landed the clerk's job at Letterkenny.

He derided it as "woman's work" and itched for something more suitable, like a mechanic's job, or working on the assembly line. But his applications always came back stamped *Not Qualified*. He was making $3.50 an hour, which came to $140 a week, which was exactly how much I was getting paid. But Rock, unlike reporters at *Public Opinion*, got time-and-a-half for overtime, and he frequently took advantage of it. He was saving so he could start a family once he got the house fixed up. He'd already done a lot of work on the place, painting and landscaping, hiring a bulldozer to fill in a low, swampy area, a grader to smooth the dirt drive. Firewood was already chopped and stacked for the coming winter.

After cashing his paycheck and making his $125 house payment that Friday, Rock visited his mother briefly, then drove to a lumberyard to buy some plywood and continued on down to the K-Mart in Hagerstown, where there was a sale on railroad ties. Rock planned to use the ties to landscape his yard, and after buying a couple dozen he headed north toward home.

But on I-81 the overloaded pickup had a blowout, just shredded a tire beyond repair. He had to shell out fifty bucks for a new tire. Fifty bucks! So on Saturday morning, head hammering, he drove back to the bank in downtown Chambersburg to get enough money to last him through the long holiday weekend.

While he was in town he stopped at Gale Diehl Sporting Goods and picked up two boxes of shells for his .300 Savage rifle. On his way home he stopped at Nichols Discount City on Lincoln Way East and bought some shotgun shells. In addition to the Savage, Rock owned 16-gauge and 12-gauge shotguns, a .22-caliber pistol, a .22 magnum rifle, and a pellet rifle. He already had more than 2,000 rounds of ammunition at his house. Asked later why he kept so much, Rock said, "Well, I was an avid hunter and I hunted and shot all the time. I bought shells like, you know, say a golfer buys golf balls, just all the time. That's my thing. That's my hobby."

WHEN ROCK GOT HOME he decided it was too hot for yard work so he blew off the railroad ties project and did a little target shooting instead. He'd nailed a paper target to a tree stump behind the house, and he stood in his front yard facing away from Black Gap Road, squeezing off half a dozen shots with the .300 Savage. The rifle was equipped with a Bush scope that magnified targets to four times their actual size. The gun had belonged to Rock's father, who died when Rock was an infant.

After a while Rock went into the house and played some more music and sat on the sofa where he'd spent the night, just relaxing, admiring the large photograph of a Technicolor sunset he'd taken while stationed in Hawaii. Then, without warning, "something happened," as he would recall later. "I just started getting into a rage . . . I just started going berserk or whatever. I started ripping up the house."

Something happened. Those two innocent words, maddeningly vague and inadequate, would become the only known motivation for the chain of events that was now in motion.

Something happened. Something snapped inside Gary Lee Rock. Something caused him to become obsessed with finding an insignificant souvenir from his Marine Corps service—a pouch that holds a magazine for an M-14 rifle. Rock didn't own an M-14, but for some unknowable reason finding that pouch was now the most important thing in his world, a matter of life and death. He started his search in the kitchen cupboards. The pouch wasn't there, so Rock sent plates and glasses smashing to the floor. He went from room to room, flipping furniture, tossing drawers, a man possessed. Still no magazine pouch.

Rock went outside and started tearing up the contents of the shed—tools, paint cans, an old refrigerator and stove—until he came upon a five-gallon jerrycan of gasoline. This brought him up short. He stared at the can. Instead of hurling it against a wall, he picked it up and, for some reason, for some unknowable reason, he started splashing gasoline around the shed. When everything was soaked, he carried the can across the lawn and into the house and continued splashing gasoline everywhere, on furniture, walls, floors, even on his precious stereo.

Then he walked back outside, struck a match, and tossed it into the shed. It went up with a *whoomp!* He re-crossed the lawn, struck another match, and tossed it into the kitchen. A much bigger *whoomp!*

Rock was instantly transfixed by what he had done. The fires spread quickly, and he felt a physical attraction to the growing flames. They looked like hands reaching into the sky, impossibly beautiful, maybe the most beautiful thing Rock had ever seen. He stood there, awe-struck, gazing at the quivering hands of fire.

Bang bang bang . . . bang bang bang bang.

Was someone shooting? Was the ammunition in the house and the shed going off? Rock didn't know for sure where the bangs were coming from. He was still mesmerized by the fire, which was close now, getting closer, getting painfully hot.

Then an explosion. Then another. Then a big gut-punch blast and a black mushroom cloud went swirling into the sky, and suddenly Rock was terrified. He ran toward the woods behind the house, startled to discover he was holding his .300 Savage rifle. He had no recollection of picking it up. But months later he was able to recall what happened next.

"I remember all the shooting going, the bangs and the explosions and stuff," Rock said, "and I looked back and the big flames were still high, and that's when I started shooting. I don't know how many times I shot. I don't even know what I was shooting at. It was like I was watching the fire and the flames were high and I just started shooting. I don't know what it was at, you know, it was like if something moved, I shot. If something moved, I shot. I just kept shooting and shooting . . . to me it wasn't reality . . . all I remember was the shooting going off. I was shooting and I was absorbed by the fire."

There were more explosions.

"I just got scared—I just got scared and I run," Rock went on. He ran with no idea where he was going. "I remember I just run and I run and I run and I run. If I fall, I get up. If I fall, I get up. I just kept running and running and running."

Finally, somewhere deep in the woods, he collapsed.

"I must have passed out because when I woke up I heard a helicopter."

WILBUR BROOKENS, a fifty-four-year-old painter who lived across Black Gap Road from Gary Lee Rock, was visiting his cousin just up the road when an explosion rattled the house. Brookens, dressed up for a big afternoon at the American Legion, hopped into his gleaming black '77 Chevy Monte Carlo, his pride and joy, the first new car he'd ever owned, and raced home. Then he sprinted across the road toward the oily smoke that was rising from the trees. As he passed his friend Russell McKenrick's house, he hollered that there was a fire, then hurried up the dirt lane. McKenrick paused to put on shoes, a delay of several seconds that probably saved his life.

When Brookens reached the crest of the narrow dirt lane, he slowed. Strange popping sounds came to him. Was the fire making those sounds? It took Brookens a moment to realize what he was hearing.

"I think they're shooting, Russ!" he shouted as his neighbor came up the lane toward him. "Get out of here!"

Another pop and McKenrick saw Brookens stiffen, saw him grab his chest, stagger, and collapse. A bullet had entered Brookens's chest, traveled through his heart, and exited out his back, killing him instantly. For someone who claimed he randomly shot and shot and shot at anything that moved, Gary Lee Rock had remarkable accuracy. And he was just getting started.

As McKenrick turned and ran, terrified and confused, he could hear sirens. When he reached Black Gap Road he saw a lime-green Chevy sedan approaching, the car of Fayetteville Volunteer Fire Department's chief, Jim Cutchall. McKenrick waved, and the car turned off the road and stopped.

"There's a man hurt back there," McKenrick told Cutchall. "Watch out, there's some trouble ahead. I just don't know what's going on."

McKenrick did not mention the possibilities that there was gunfire or that Brookens had been shot. Cutchall didn't say a word. He drove toward the fire, reaching for his microphone.

JEAN COVERT, THE HICK from the sticks who found her niche as a reporter in the big city of Chambersburg, had joined the Fayetteville Volunteer Fire Department in the spring of that year. Women were not widely welcome in volunteer fire departments in Pennsylvania in those days, but Fayetteville's was not a typical department. It was led by thirty-three-year-old James W. Cutchall, who had instituted major reforms in his four years as chief, including the notion, then radical in the macho world of firefighting, that women could do the job every bit as well as men. Cutchall believed this so strongly, in fact, that he'd pulled his department out of a fiercely competitive pumping contest a year earlier when one of his female firefighters, on a rules technicality, was disqualified from operating the pump.

Beyond such symbolic gestures, though, Chutchall had helped build an impressive organization, expanding a fledgling junior program for thirteen- to eighteen-year-old boys and girls, buying new equipment, expanding the fire house, establishing a scholarship fund, and demanding a peak level of professionalism from every one of his firefighters at all times, no exceptions, no excuses. I'd interviewed Cutchall in January of that year about a rigorous new training program he was drawing up for the area's ambulance crews. "An ambulance doesn't save your life," he told me. "It transports you to the hospital. That's all." For Jim Cutchall, that was not nearly good enough.

I came away from that interview impressed by the man's passion and intensity. He reminded me of Bob Collins—a born leader who had a gift for making his troops want to outdo themselves. Those who knew Cutchall—and everyone seemed to know this local boy who'd graduated from Shippensburg State College, married a local girl, and was now in charge of the commercial loan department at Farmers & Merchants Bank, a sure bet to become president of the bank one day—everyone described him as driven, demanding, a perfectionist. If volunteer fire companies serve as secular churches in small American towns like Fayetteville, then Jim Cutchall was this church's undisputed high priest.

While the rest of the company performed routine maintenance chores on that hot Saturday morning, Jean Covert was in the chief's office discussing the upcoming "Firefighters Almost Anything Goes" fundraiser the department was sponsoring, a spinoff of the popular NBC game show that pitted residents of small towns against each other in zany competitions like swing relays and pie-throwing contests. Jeanie, a shameless civic cheerleader, was a proud member of the Chambersburg team that had won the 1976 national title.

Given what was about to become known, it's possible that Jean Covert and Jim Cutchall were discussing something far more serious than pie-throwing contests that Saturday morning.

When a call came for an ambulance to respond to a car accident on Lincoln Way East shortly after noon, Jean and the chief hurried from his office. On the way to his car he turned to her and said, "Stay here now. I may need you later."

Though it was a routine call, Jean was disappointed by the order, almost angry. It would be the first time she didn't respond to a call from one of her two privileged positions—either the passenger seat of the chief's car, or sitting in the cab of the fire engine between the driver and lead officer.

The chief's Chevy sedan turned right on Main Street and headed west toward the accident, followed by the ambulance. Before the dispatcher could repeat the call, in keeping with emergency protocol, he issued a call for a structure fire on Black Gap Road. As firefighters scrambled aboard Engine 7-1, they saw the chief's Chevy heading east, toward Black Gap Road. Passing the fire house, Cutchall waved to Engine 7-1 as it was pulling out of its berth, like an officer signaling for the cavalry to follow him into battle.

Jean didn't hesitate. She went to her car and slid behind the wheel as three firefighters piled in with her. She followed Engine 7-1 at a safe distance as it moved east along Main Street, then turned north.

At the fire scene, Jean grabbed her camera and walked up the dirt lane, eager to find out what the chief wanted her to do. She was there both as a reporter/photographer for *Public Opinion* and as the fire department's official photographer. One of Jim Cutchall's innovations was to begin building a photographic record of all incidents the department responded to, large or small. Jean noticed blood on the chief's car, but she saw no sign of him, and she didn't see Wilbur Brookens's body in the lane as she walked toward the clearing and started snapping pictures of the burning house.

When she got within fifty feet of the flames, someone shouted for her to get back behind the fire engine. It was then that she saw the shattered passenger window of the chief's car, the bullet holes in the windshield of Engine 7-1. She spotted Raymond Rotz, president of the department, and she went to him to find out what had become of the chief.

Bob Cox and Ken Peiffer of *The Waynesboro Record Herald* had just arrived on the scene. When they spotted a familiar state police lieutenant, they approached him and asked what was going on. "It's that damn Hessian in-breeding," came the sardonic reply. The reporters noticed Jean Covert standing nearby, talking to Ray Rotz. Then they watched, astonished, as Jean wobbled, fainted, and crumpled to the ground. Cox scooped her up in his arms and carried her to Black Gap Road, out of harm's way.

AFTER LISTENING TO RUSSELL McKenrick's vague warning at the end of the dirt lane, Jim Cutchall eased his Chevy toward the fire. "Chief 7 to headquarters," he said into the microphone.

"Chief 7," the radio dispatcher replied.

"Advise Engine 7-1 to lay out from the roadway back up the lane. We have a house fully engulfed."

Hearing the command on their radio, all seven firefighters aboard Engine 7-1 knew what to do. The driver, Assistant Chief Bob Monn, turned off Black Gap Road and hit the brakes as firefighter Charles Hoffman hopped off the tailboard, grabbed the end of a hose, and secured it around a tree. As Monn eased the engine up the lane, the hose unfurled from the back end. Hoffman's assignment was to wait and hook the hose up to the pumper truck that was on its way.

Monn and Sergeant Bill Kady, seated beside him in the cab, heard the chief's voice crackle over the radio. "Chief 7 to headquarters. Dispatch me an ambulance and a—"

Then nothing. Odd, but Monn and Kady had a lot on their minds. Monn had to drive slowly, weaving the hulking truck between the trees that lined the narrow lane. He and Kady could see flames through the trees, and when they got to the top of the ridge they could see the chief's car parked off to the left, but no sign of the chief. They could hear the crackle of a downed electrical wire that was writhing like an angry snake. There was a man lying in the lane. Monn, unable to get around the prone body, brought the engine to a stop.

"And everything started happening in milli-seconds," Monn would say later. "There was crackling going on and some more popping and then it seemed like stuff came in the windshield or something—we didn't know what was going on—and I guess at some point I put it together that it was more than accidental bullets coming in the windshield. I figured we're being shot at. So I told Bill to get down. At that point I didn't even have time to set the parking brake on the engine. I got out and started to tell everybody to get down and get out of here—and the engine started to roll forward. So I had to run up and pull the parking brake."

Though Monn didn't realize it at the time, a bullet had grazed his right arm.

"I think I remember seeing a silhouette of some sort," he continued. "I never actually saw a clear view of a person. And you could hear the popping then, you could hear the gun going off – *poom! poompoom! poom!* . . . I ran as hard as I could out the driveway because at that time we didn't have portable radios, and the only radio was in the engine and the engine was being shot at. So I ran as hard as I could to the hard road because there was an engine there and I could get to a radio."

Monn grabbed the microphone and barked, "Headquarters, stand by! Dispatch PSP (Pennsylvania State Police) to the scene of the shooting!" After the dispatcher ordered all units to clear the air, Monn continued, "I want the police on the scene! Emergency! We have some people shot at, it's ah, ah . . . Give me some help over here, we're in a hell of a shape . . . We've got guns going off, people shot. Dispatch me three ambulances to the scene."

MINUTES EARLIER, JIM CUTCHALL had said into his microphone, "Dispatch me an ambulance and a—"

The first bullet caught Cuthcall in his right forearm and lodged there. The force of the impact knocked the microphone out of his hand, spun him to the right. The second bullet hit just above his left ear, bullet fragments spraying through his throat and into the right side of his brain. Cutchall managed to open the driver's door, but he spilled to the ground and rolled onto his back. Two more bullets hit the car. Then the shooting stopped.

SCOTT REICHENBACH, EIGHTEEN YEARS OLD and freshly graduated from Chambersburg Area Senior High School, was riding to Black Gap Road in the jump seat of Engine 7-1, his back toward Sergeant Bill Kady. Scott was a big, strong, shaggy kid who had become a junior member of the department in 1973, the year Jim Cutchall became chief. For the past two years, after qualifying as an emergency medical technician, Scott had been living at the fire house full-time, riding the ambulance at night and responding to fires during the day when he wasn't in school. He loved firefighting so much he planned to do it for the rest of his life.

As Engine 7-1 turned off Black Gap Road and eased up the drive, Scott turned around and crouched to look over Bill Kady's shoulder through the windshield. The sight of a man lying in the lane didn't surprise Scott. He'd responded to many emergencies where people suffered heart attacks or other serious injuries. He could see flames roaring out of the windows and the front of the house, the place cooking, but his primary concern was the downed electrical line, arcing, spitting sparks.

Got to keep an eye on that, he told himself. The engine stopped just short of the fallen man.

"All of a sudden," Scott recalled later, "bullet holes start to form in the windshield, but it didn't register with me. I'm not a hunter. The guys in the front seats, Bill and Bobby, they dove to the floor. When I stood up to look at this wire that's dancing around, that's when the bullet hit me and shot me back."

Scott felt scorching pain.

"I've never been stabbed before, but that's what it felt like. I don't know if you've ever seen stories about warriors where they talk about how everything slows down. That's a true phenomenon and I experienced that. I actually could look down and see the fibers of my coat separate and flutter. And it just felt like the bullet went through in slow motion. If I was to take a knife out and run it through your arm and pull it back, that would be what it would feel like. It felt like being stabbed. And once the pain arrived, all of a sudden I felt this real loud *snap* . . . and then everything went back to full speed."

Part of the bullet had passed through Scott's right arm and banged off the hose box behind him.

"I bounced forward and my hand is laying on the seat and my arm looks like it's twice as long as it was. My hand is farther away than it should be. I can see my fingers curling up real slow—and I wasn't doing it. So my first assumption was that my arm had come off, it was blown off . . . I remember reaching down and grabbing my wrist with my left hand and putting my face into the seat to hide myself. I didn't want to leave my arm there. The first thing that come to my mind was, if this guy's shooting at us he could walk right up here and shoot me. If somebody was gonna shoot me, I at least wanted to give myself a chance. I didn't want somebody coming up and sticking a gun in my face. And honestly, this is no lie, I'm not trying to be macho,

I stepped off the fire truck and *walked* away. Don't ask me why. Wouldn't you think I'd take off running, to get the hell out of there? I walked to the back of the fire truck. He shot at me again on my way back. Psychologically, of everything that happened that day, that was the thing that stuck with me the most— the one that missed. It missed right here." He touched his right ear. "I felt that. It sounded like a bumblebee going by at a thousand miles an hour. I felt the velocity of the bullet move my ear. And if you remember anything about this story, Jim Cutchall was shot right here." He touched his neck just behind the ear. "That's what he was aiming for. He just missed me by that much. If you ever want to hear what it sounds like to get shot at, watch the movie *Saving Private Ryan*, when they're on Normandy Beach. When you hear that buzzing sound, that's as close as I've ever heard anybody do that sound."

When he got to the back of the fire truck, Scott came upon Kady and John Furry, who'd ridden on the tailboard with Charles Hoffman.

"I'm hit," Scott told them.

"Look," Kady said, "it's still attached so you're all right. Just go back over the hill as far as you can. Jim's hit too, really bad. We're going to try to get him out."

Following his sergeant's orders, Scott walked over the rise in the lane, then he walked into the woods and lay down. His experience on the ambulance crew kicked in, and he set about assessing his wound. He took off his coat and was relieved to see that his right arm was still attached, though it was swelling and had a grapefruit-sized hole in it. Bones were sticking out. He could hear bullets buzzing through the trees, bumblebees traveling at a thousand miles an hour.

When an emergency crew arrived and knelt down to tend to him, Scott told them to go take care of the chief, that Sergeant Kady said he was hit really bad. The crew

SOMETHING HAPPENED   149

left him with several Kotex, and he set about stanching his own wound.

"That's when Bill and John went to get Jim," Scott said. "I can't imagine doing that. Honestly, people say about heroes and stuff—volunteer firemen to go under fire to get their brother? I don't know if I coulda done that."

Bill Kady and John Furry had started crawling on the ground on the left side of Engine 7-1. When they reached the left front tire, they paused. They could see the chief lying on his back under his car's open door. He wasn't moving. The space between the engine and the chief's car would give the sniper a clear shot. Kady called to Cutchall. No response. He called again. Nothing.

"I was scared shitless," Kady said later, but he forced himself to crawl across the open space. He could feel the heat from the burning house, but he didn't hear any more shots. When he reached the chief, Kady immediately saw the bullet hole in his head. It was bad, but the chief was still alive. Kady spoke into Cutchall's ear, but again got no response. Suddenly, John Furry was there, and together they dragged the chief across the treacherous open space to relative safety behind the fire truck.

Jeff Probst, an emergency medical technician, arrived and began to perform mouth-to-mouth resuscitation on Cutchall. Another ambulance had arrived, and the firefighters slid their chief onto a spine board and loaded him into the ambulance. It had large side-view mirrors, and the driver, Paul Etter, was having trouble turning around in such tight quarters. Seeing him struggle, Bob Monn shouted, "Fuck the mirrors! Just get it turned around!"

After snapping off both mirrors, Etter got the ambulance turned around and raced to Chambersburg Hospital. Cutchall was alive when the ambulance arrived at the hospital at 1:10 p.m. Doctors immediately went to work on him, but it was hopeless. Twenty minutes later they pronounced Jim Cutchall dead.

SCOTT REICHENBACH WAS ABOUT TO go into surgery when he got the news. "I remember going into the emergency room and Bobby Monn was the first one to tell me Chief Cutchall had died. Then Dr. Ashby came in—they alerted him because he was a M*A*S*H doctor in Korea and he was a specialist in gunshot wounds. I remember them constantly giving me injections, three different shots in each leg. That was the worst thing, and I'm not exaggerating, having twenty needles stuck in me. When Dr. Ashby come in, that's when I remember that he started lifting my arm up and looking and I could hear the blood go *splat* on the floor. And then they put me out."

WHEN GARY LEE ROCK WAS awakened by the throb of the helicopter, he got another surprise: though he had no recollection of changing out of the clothes he'd worn to last night's cookout, he was now dressed for war. He was wearing his Marine fatigue pants and combat boots and dog tags. His pockets were bulging with ammunition. He also had canteens, a large knife, a shotgun, and the .300 Savage. He was shirtless. He had no idea where he was, but in his mind he could still see the flaming hands reaching into the sky, and he could remember shooting.

The helicopter was making sweeps, a sound Rock knew well from the Marine Corps, the sound of a trained crew methodically searching for someone. He climbed a tree, hoping to get his bearings, but all he could see was faceless, unfamiliar mountains. He decided to walk downhill, figuring he would come out of the woods eventually. He knew something was wrong.

He walked for hours, until he hit a trail that led to a clearing, a large, well-tended lawn that fronted a snug cabin, its porch supported by five wooden pillars. The property was known as Conococheague Camp. Rock, exhausted, sat down and leaned back against a tree. The sun had set, and dusk was seeping in. In the failing light Rock could see an older man sitting on the cabin's porch.

W. Scott Heisey was drinking a cup of coffee and smoking a cigarette on the porch when he heard a noise in the woods. Most likely a deer, Heisey thought. But it turned out to be a man, naked to the waist. He was dragging something, some sort of stick. The man's chest was laced with bloody scrapes, as though he'd been through heavy brush. Must be a hiker who got lost, Heisey thought, watching him flop against a tree, clearly exhausted. When the man stood up and moved to another tree closer to the house, Heisey saw that the stick was a rifle. Then it hit him: this was the man he'd been hearing about all afternoon on the news, the man the State Police were after.

Heisey called softly to his wife Dot, and she telephoned the police, who ordered the couple to lie on the floor and stay on the line after Dot gave directions to the camp. Within minutes, two troopers arrived, followed by more. They kept coming, bristling with guns, leading bloodhounds, and soon Gary Lee Rock was surrounded.

"State police!" someone shouted. "Put the gun down!"

Rock didn't put the gun down. He rested the rifle's barrel under his chin and put his right index finger on the trigger. "How many people are dead?" he asked.

"I don't know," said one trooper.

"What difference does it make?" said another.

It made a world of difference to Rock. As he would explain later, "I didn't want to give myself up until I knew what happened. I was at the point where I was on the edge, you know. If they would have told me I killed two people, then that would have been it. I would've blew my head off."

The conversation shifted. One trooper offered to buy Rock a six pack of beer. Another made small talk about the Marine Corps. Another asked if Rock wanted to see his mother. The answer was no, definitely not, but he would be willing to talk with his sister Kathy.

With the last daylight leaking away, the police brought in floodlights and trained them on Rock. Soon his sister arrived, and for the next hour she made small talk, reassuring her brother, urging him to put down the gun and surrender. He kept asking how many people he'd killed, and he vowed he was not going to spend the rest of his life in a cage.

Suddenly, Rock hurled his rifle toward the troopers and, holding only the knife, sprinted for the tree line. A blast from a 12-gauge shotgun knocked him to the ground. Troopers scrambled to handcuff their suspect, ending one of the largest manhunts in state history.

Bob Collins, who had spent the afternoon covering the story with half a dozen *Public Opinion* staffers, was at the end of the lane that led in to the camp, held there by police who refused to let reporters get any closer to the tense standoff. It was an anxious group—everyone aware that an armed killer was somewhere in the dark woods nearby.

"At 10:01 p.m., reporters standing at a police barricade on Stillhouse Hollow Road heard a shot," Collins would write in his account of events. "A trooper at the house called into the radio: 'He just bought himself . . . subject is wounded, send an ambulance.'"

Hearing the radio report, David Scott Smith hurried to Chambersburg Hospital, hoping to beat the ambulance there. Though David had no way of knowing it, Rock had not been seriously wounded by the shotgun blast, and when troopers loaded him into a cruiser for the ride to the hospital, the suspect was conscious and lucid. Rock remarked to the troopers that his handcuffs were on wrong. He had handcuffed a lot of men in the Marines, he said, and the keyhole was supposed to be toward the prisoner's body so he couldn't reach it with a key and escape. The keyhole on Rock's handcuffs was facing outward. The troopers in the car made a note of this remark. Coupled with Rock's repeated questions about the number of dead, they took this to mean the suspect was sane and very much aware of what he had done. Rock's sister was sitting beside him in the back seat. His brother-in-law, sitting in front with two troopers, kept telling Rock to shut up.

When the cruiser reached the hospital, Rock walked across the loading dock, his sister holding his left arm, a man on his right. When they pushed through the doors that led to the emergency room, David was ready, and he started snapping his Nikon as fast as he could. The contact sheet he showed me later looked like a series of movie stills: the door swings open; Rock enters,

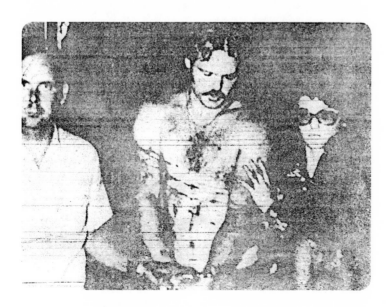

shirtless, flanked by a woman and a man, his hands cuffed in front of him, eyes downcast, arms and chest striped with bloody cuts. As the trio approaches, the woman spots the camera, and her left hand comes toward the lens, hits it. The next shots are of the ceiling and walls as David is jolted by the blow. But he got one magnificent spot news picture.

By the time Gary Lee Rock went into surgery that night, the story was national news. I don't remember how I heard the news, but even for someone without a telephone or a radio, even for someone who rarely watched television news, the story would have been hard to miss. Everyone was talking about it, and print, radio, and wire service reporters were swarming in, along with TV news vans. The circus had come to town.

The story made the NBC Sunday Night News the following day, and by then Bob Collins had given me my marching orders. As part of our saturation coverage of the shootings and their aftermath, my job was to get into Chambersburg Hospital somehow and interview the wounded firefighter Scott Reichenbach.

Collins had gone into full combat mode, orchestrating our coverage with the precision of a military campaign. Every staffer who had not left town for the holiday weekend was pressed into service, and we all understood that we were working against stiff competition and some colossal bad timing. The fire and shootings happened minutes after the Saturday paper hit the street, we didn't publish on Sunday, and there would be no paper on Monday, the Fourth of July. That meant we wouldn't put out a paper until noon Tuesday—an eternity even in the pre-24/7 news cycle of those days. We would have to figure out angles that made stale news seem fresh. It was a daunting assignment, but Gary Lee Rock, a man of endless surprises, was about to do us a huge favor.

DOCTORS AT CHAMBERSBURG HOSPITAL removed shotgun pellets from Gary Lee Rock and treated his minor cuts on Saturday night. The next day, shortly after noon, Rock was arraigned in his hospital room on two counts of criminal homicide. Then for security—for Rock's security—he was transported to the State Correctional Institution in Camp Hill, near Harrisburg.

The next morning, the Fourth of July, Rock emerged from a deep, narcoticized sleep to the sound of a radio. It was tuned to a newscast. Ex-Marine Gary Lee Rock, the newscaster was saying, had been charged with the murders of Fayetteville fire chief James Cutchall and Fayetteville resident Wilbur Brookens.

Rock made a snap decision: "I just decided there wasn't anything more to stay around for."

He then reached for the IV bottle that was feeding fluids into his arm, smashed it on a windowsill, and began slashing his arm and neck with the jagged glass. The sound of breaking glass brought prison guards rushing into the room, and they wrestled the bottle from Rock. It took thirty-three stitches—thirteen in his neck and twenty in his arm—to close the gashes.

The newspaper gods had smiled on *Public Opinion* after all and given us fresh news to report on Tuesday. Dawn DeCwikiel-Kane's story appeared under a banner headline: "Rock attempts suicide."

AT ABOUT THE TIME Gary Lee Rock was trying to kill himself, I was riding an elevator to the third floor in Chambersburg Hospital. I remember feeling a sickening sense of dread. Not only was I sure that other reporters had beaten me to Scott Reichenbach, I was now part of a media circus, whether I liked it or not. But far worse, I felt queasy about interviewing a young man who had so narrowly survived a brush with death. This was beyond invasive; this was heartless, nearly ghoulish. In my mind, I had a picture of Scott Reichenbach: he would be a perfectly average, perfectly happy teenager who, through a freakish flash of violence, was being elevated against his will to the ephemeral status of newsmaker. And I was there to do the unwelcome elevating.

The scene inside Room 380 did nothing to dispel my dread. The room was full of flowers, and there on the bed lay Scott Reichenbach, his shattered arm swaddled in a bulky, elevated cast. His face, considering the circumstances, was surprisingly sunny. I was struck by how boyish he looked, way too young and innocent to be subjected to an ordeal like this—not only the terror and agony of getting shot, but then having to sit through the prying questions of a stranger with a notebook.

Scott had the guarded, overly polite manners country people often use as a way of deflecting the advances of strangers. I had to pull the quotes out of him. I figured he was tired of rehashing the story for friends and family and other reporters, but eventually I got him to tell me a bit of his personal history, then recount what happened when he arrived at the fire scene, the shock of realizing he'd been shot, the aftermath. He said his big hope was that he would be in good enough shape to attend Chief Cutchall's funeral on Wednesday. A stream of firefighters, family members, and well-wishers passed through the room while I tried to conduct the interview, a maddening distraction.

I left that hospital room thinking I finally knew how it felt to be part of a pack. I remembered that picture of my father pouring coffee in *The Washington Post* newsroom on a long-ago election night, and now I understood my aversion to the relief on those men's faces. Gary Lee Rock's crime was not one of those canned news events that come along at prescribed intervals; this was spot news, random, unpredictable, almost unimaginable. Yet, this spot news story had something in common with canned news: it had attracted the full three-ring media circus, and every reporter I encountered in Chambersburg that week was glowing with the same gratitude I'd seen on the faces of my father's colleagues. As long as this story kept unfolding, they wouldn't have to think for themselves.

Driving back to the paper to write my story, I realized I'd used Scott Reichenbach just as readily as I'd used Merle Unger's mother in that Maryland courthouse while a jury deliberated her son's fate. *Writers are always selling somebody out.* But this was different, I told myself. I was the only reporter on hand to relate the anguish Merle Unger's mother was going through, and it seemed important to give that voiceless woman a chance to speak. Driving away from the hospital now, I thought I knew how it felt to be one more hyena ripping a shred of news from an unwilling source. There was no other way to put it: being part of a pack made me feel unclean.

Only trouble was, I had it all exactly wrong.

IN MARCH OF 2015, I sat down with Scott Reichenbach at his kitchen table in Fayetteville, a few miles from the spot where he'd nearly died thirty-eight years earlier. Scott was fifty-five now, still big and shaggy, but his youthful guardedness had given way to a warm and booming gregariousness. I felt instantly welcome. He had recently retired from his post as assistant fire chief with the Defense Logistics Agency in New Cumberland, Pennsylvania. So he'd done what few people manage to do: he had lived out his youthful dream and spent his life as a firefighter.

After offering me a beer, Scott brought out a fat album of newspaper clippings from the Fourth of July weekend in 1977. Some anonymous citizen had collected the clips, then donated them to the nearby Mont Alto

Fire Department, which passed them along to Scott. There were articles from *Public Opinion*, including my front-page interview with Scott, as well as stories from papers in Philadelphia, Baltimore, Harrisburg, Hagerstown, and dozens more—the fruit of the pack's labor, in black and white.

I turned on a tape recorder, a tool I rarely use, and after getting Scott to relive the events of July 2, 1977, I got him to tell me the story I most wanted to hear: his version of what happened when I came to interview him in Room 380 at Chambersburg Hospital on the Fourth of July.

"I didn't know what to say to you," he began. "I really hadn't taken time to process everything yet. Everything happened so fast—you're put out, they're working on you, and of course your concern is your family and the Cutchall family and the fire house. How are we going to survive? I really didn't think about the incident much until you asked me about it. And then I had to start processing all that stuff."

"Do you remember how that felt?" I asked. "Here's my memory: you seemed very uncomfortable."

"I don't know if I was uncomfortable, or confused. Up until that point, everybody had come in and asked, 'How ya doin'?' 'You okay?'—talking to you about your well-being. Of course back then there were rumors. As a matter of fact, my girlfriend told me that one of her friends attending the Scotland Fair called to say it was going around the fairgrounds that I'd died. That's the kind of stuff you were listening to at the time. And when you sat down with me, that was the first time anybody said, 'Tell me exactly what happened.' And then I had to start thinking through my memory of what exactly happened. It was all pretty vivid—and honestly, that was probably the first opportunity I had to mentally recover a little bit. I've never been afraid to talk about that incident. Some

guys go to war and they're in battle and they hold everything inside of 'em and it eats away at 'em. It was probably the first step in the healing process, getting it out of
my head and talking about it, telling somebody exactly
how you felt and what you went through. Here we are,
forty years later, doing it again, and it's just as healing
now as it was then. You were the first person, including
my family, who heard it from me, what I experienced at
that particular moment in my life."

"So," I said, "this was the first chance you had to
heal through talking about it?"

"Right."

The pack hadn't beaten me to Scott's hospital room
after all. I'd gotten an exclusive interview and didn't
even know it. I said, "My recollection was that I felt like
I was invading, like I was violating something. Here you
are, shot up, probably on some pretty strong pain medi-
cine, and I felt really uncomfortable going into that room
and talking to you. Partly because of the media circus
that was going on in town, but also because that's a
very invasive thing to do. I'm glad I did it, I'm glad we
talked, but I walked away feeling like, man, that was
rough. That's harsh to go into a room with a kid who's
just been shot and start asking him questions. And now
you're telling me it helped, it was healing."

"Yeah. The other thing I remember thinking, before
the interview, is 'How am I going to put this in layman's
terms?' Because we use slang in the fire service, just
like other groups do. I knew I was going to have to explain a lot of stuff to you, and I didn't know if I really
wanted to explain." He laughed.

"I have a completely different memory of what happened in that hospital room," I said.

"It wasn't until after you left that I thought about
how that really felt good to lay that all out to somebody,"
Scott said, "especially somebody who has no idea what

firefighters do on a day-to-day basis. So I was able to get a lot of things off my chest, and you were the very first one I was able to tell the whole story to . . . That's another thing, I've talked to so many people about this incident over the years, but I've never discussed it with Bobby Monn or Bill Kady or anybody else who was on that truck. We've never sat down and talked about what we experienced as a group. Never."

"Why do you think that is?"

"I don't know. When you grow up in the fire service, you don't sit around and talk about the bad stuff. If you dwell on the bad stuff, it'll eat you alive."

I had one last question. "Did you ever wish for vengeance against Gary Lee Rock? And how have your feelings changed over time?"

"I didn't have any feelings of vengeance toward him. I figured if he rotted the rest of his life in jail, that would be worse punishment than executing him. I was more interested in the psychology of the whole thing. What caused him to snap? What was going through his head?"

I LEFT SCOTT'S HOUSE that day feeling something that went beyond exoneration. I'd spent nearly forty years believing I'd been heartless in the performance of my job only to learn that I'd inadvertently helped begin a process of healing that's still going on today. What a surprise, what a remarkable gift. Strange how we stumble onto hidden truths. Strange how we can be released from feeling unclean, without warning, and made to realize that for all those years we actually had every reason to feel proud.

Love Child

While I was in Mercersburg on Tuesday covering Tim Rockwell's press conference, Scott Reichenbach was forcing himself to walk up and down the third-floor hallways at Chambersburg Hospital, determined to prove to the staff that he was strong enough to attend Chief Cutchall's funeral. The next morning his doctors cleared him to go—provided he rode in a wheelchair.

I spent that blistering Wednesday afternoon walking alongside Engine 7-1 as it carried Cutchall's flower-covered casket from the high school to Lincoln Cemetery. The town was thronged with spectators, with reporters and cops and firefighters from Franklin County and from neighboring counties and states. Bob Collins had pulled out all the stops and hired a helicopter so we could get aerial shots of the sprawling extravaganza. Its incessant buzzing, along with the crowds and the punishing heat, scraped my nerves raw.

As I walked alongside the casket, I snapped pictures and interviewed dozens of spectators, producing a short, impressionistic sketch of the stunned mood along the funeral route. My story about Tim Rockwell's plan to challenge Bill Shuman was buried on that day's local news page, which was where it belonged, along with my very minor story about a new subdivision ordinance in the hamlet of Little Cove. These last two stories, though trifling compared to the big news of the day, were hugely reassuring to me. They proved that I was distancing myself from the pack even before it had left town.

Jean Covert wasn't so lucky. She was one of the last people to see Jim Cutchall alive and one of the first to arrive at the scene of his murder, and Bob Collins wasn't about to miss out on this juicy exclusive. Despite Jean's protests, Collins wanted—no, he demanded—that she write a first-person account of what she saw on that traumatic Saturday. Marie Lanser remembers watching Collins force Jean into one of the glass-walled cubicles that ran along the back wall of the newsroom, ordering her to sit down and write. Under different circumstances, Collins had once given Marie the same orders. Jean was clearly distraught, and Marie remembers it as a "brutal" scene. And this was before Marie or anyone else knew the whole story.

Jean's first-person account appeared in a box on the front page of Wednesday's paper, under the headline "If chief had not told me to stay . . . I would have been in car with him." The story made the point that if Jean had ridden to the fire in one of her two customary spots—in the passenger seat of Cutchall's car or the cab of Engine 7-1—she almost certainly would have suffered a fatal gunshot wound. So it seemed to be a story about luck, fate, and the road not taken. Jean wrote that only after snapping pictures of Gary Lee Rock's burning house did she notice the shattered passenger window in Cutchall's car and the bullet holes in the windshield of the fire truck. "Without having time to realize what those revealed to me," she wrote, "department President Raymond Rotz told me the chief had died."

The shock of the news was what caused Jean to faint, which inspired Bob Cox to gallantly scoop her up and carry her down the lane to safety. Her story ended with this loaded line: "The anger and disappointment I felt that Saturday afternoon because I could not go have been replaced by a thankful prayer to the man who gave me my life."

As the rest of us in the newsroom were about to learn, Jim Cutchall gave Jean Covert much more than her life.

Dawn DeCwikiel-Kane was one of the first to hear the news. After the media circus finally left town and life tried to return to normal, Dawn and Jean went to lunch one day at the Pizza Hut. Recalling that lunch nearly forty years later, Dawn still couldn't hide her shock.

"Jean told me she was pregnant and Jim Cutchall was the father of her child," Dawn said. "I remember being upset, and I was just stunned. Back in the newsroom I told Katy, but Katy already knew."

Soon everyone in the newsroom knew that Jim Cutchall, the happily married pillar of the community, had left behind a dark secret. Inevitably, word got around town. Just as inevitably, there were people who refused to believe that Cutchall could have fathered a child out of wedlock.

As it turned out, Jean was already in her second trimester when Cutchall was murdered, and she gave birth to a healthy baby boy in November. She named him Jaime in honor of his father. With Jean's mother providing day care, Jean was able to return to work soon after the birth. From time to time she brought Jaime into the newsroom to show him off—the scarlet letter was not in Jean's alphabet—and the boy would sit on her desk, pounding gleefully on her typewriter. Though no one knew it at the time, a future *Public Opinion* reporter had been born.

The Man Who Wasn't There

Scott Reichenbach's question was on everyone's mind: Why? Why did Gary Lee Rock perform acts that were not only out of character, but nearly beyond imagining? What was the something that happened inside this seemingly ordinary young man? What was the thing that snapped, turning the quiet guy next door into a crazed arsonist and murderer?

People need to be able to grasp a motive for monstrous acts so they can reassure themselves that such acts, however horrific, are understandable aberrations from the established order. It is unbearable for most people to ponder the possibility that monstrous acts can occur without a graspable motive, without reason, randomly, out of nowhere—or that such acts can be committed by absolutely anyone. Most people simply cannot abide the fact that we are all, given the right circumstances, capable of the monstrous.

And so people began looking for Gary Lee Rock's motive in all the obvious places. He grew up without a father. He was disappointed by his experience in the Marine Corps. He hated his demeaning job and was frustrated by his failure to win a promotion. He was hurt when one girlfriend left him and hurt again when he saw Ann Chestnut with another guy at a party. The blowout on I-81 and the $50 replacement tire were yet another setback in his thwarted desire to make a home and start a family—to live the American dream. But even as people went through this predictable litany, it was obvious none of it could begin to account for what Rock had done. Clearly, a more nuanced explanation was needed.

A story in *Public Opinion* on July 5, written by Margie Uhrich, performed the obligatory background check on the accused killer. Margie talked to all the usual suspects: Rock's friends, bosses, co-workers, neighbors, and teachers. They told her the same things people say whenever someone commits a shocking act of violence: Rock was "a loner," "a quiet kind of guy," "really dependable," "easy-going," "fairly bright." None of it was enlightening. It wasn't until Margie talked to some of Rock's high school teachers that her article moved beyond boilerplate:

> But many of the CASHS teachers contacted yesterday didn't remember teaching a Gary Rock in their classes.
>
> "If it's the same person I'm thinking of, he was a very quiet person that always stuck to his business," said Glenn Crouse, an English teacher.
>
> But many responses resembled that of Anthony Memmi: "I don't remember him, and I've talked to several teachers who don't remember him."

I don't remember him. Now here's something worth knowing. Gary Lee Rock was average in every way: average height (5' 10"), average weight (160 pounds), average education from an average (or slightly below-average) high school, average ambitions (work a lot of overtime, fix the house, start a family). He was not one of those people who leaves a lasting impression. But Rock went beyond being merely forgettable all the way to becoming invisible. He was the spookiest, most unsettling type. He was the man who wasn't there.

The novelist Don DeLillo has spent his decorated career dissecting such characters. A classic of the type was Lee Harvey Oswald, ex-Marine, presumed assassin of President John F. Kennedy, and the central character in DeLillo's 1988 novel *Libra*. As DeLillo told an interviewer when the novel was published, he sees the violent acts of men like Oswald as a response to their marginal lives, what DeLillo calls "life in small rooms," with the implication that those stultifying rooms are sprinkled throughout the opulent mansion known as Life in America. I believe Gary Lee Rock lived in such a small room, invisible to the world, desperate to break out and be seen, and this fact is the closest we'll ever come to a motive for his violent outburst.

Referring to Oswald, DeLillo said:

> His life in small rooms is the antithesis of the life America seems to promise its citizens . . . I see contemporary violence as a kind of sardonic response to the promise of consumer fulfillment in America. Again, we come back to these men in small rooms who can't get out and who have to organize their desperation and their loneliness, who have to give it a destiny and who often end up doing this through violent means. I see this desperation against the backdrop of brightly colored packages and products and consumer happiness and every promise that American life makes day by day and minute by minute everywhere we go.

I believe this map of Oswald's path to an act of astonishing violence is equally valid for Rock. Or maybe DeLillo and I are guilty of wishful thinking. Maybe this is a flimsy way of denying the fact that certain human acts cannot be explained or understood. The Norwegian novelist Karl Ove Knausgaard came to this conclusion when he tried to grasp what drove his countryman, Anders Breivik, to detonate a car bomb in Oslo in

2011, killing eight people, before driving to the island of Utøya, where he spent more than an hour methodically shooting sixty-nine more, mostly young people attending a summer camp, many of them at point-blank range. Writing in *The New Yorker*, Knausgaard posed a familiar question: "What can prompt a relatively well-functioning man to do something so horrific?"

Knausgaard's initial theory, based on a 1,500-page manifesto and YouTube video disseminated by Breivik, was that he was on a one-man mission to save Norway from "the Muslim invasion." Knausgaard notes that news commentators described Anders Breivik as "small, petty, pathetic," adjectives that could be applied without much of a stretch to Gary Lee Rock. Knausgaard goes on to reject the personal history of the killer as adequate motivation for his crimes—his absent father, his negligent mother, his narcissism and political extremism, his inability to empathize with others. Plenty of people have such histories and personality traits, Knausgaard notes, and they don't wind up murdering seventy-seven people. The closest Knausgaard comes to a motive is this: "He wanted to be seen; that is what drove him, nothing else. Look at me. Look at me. Look at me . . . Breivik remained unseen, and it destroyed him." In the end, Knausgaard rejects even this small consolation. The title of his essay is chilling because it calls Breivik's—and Rock's—crimes precisely what they are: "The Inexplicable."

KNAUSGAARD'S FRUITLESS SEARCH for Breivik's motivation pointed out another fact that has been haunting me as I've been writing this book. What's shocking is that the slaughter of seventy-seven people is no longer shocking. "The most striking aspect of the ten-week trial," as Knausgaard put it, "is how normalized both the perpetrator and the crime had become."

One of the reasons I wanted to write this book was a desire to recreate the cumulative effect of the events I heard about, witnessed, or covered in a specific place at a specific time in my life at the outset of my writing career. The litany of those events still staggers me—shunning, kidnapping, rape, arson, murder, attempted suicide, the paranormal, the birth of a love child, the death of my mother. I can remember that there were times when it all seemed like too much to bear. Franklin County's postcard prettiness surely contributed to the "disconnect" Marie Lanser mentioned, the jarring, almost otherworldly way these events worked on me and, I'm sure, on the rest of the paper's staff.

I was not yet twenty-five years old at the time, but I was aware that violence has always been a staple of American life. I believed I was living through what Walker Percy called the "dread latter days of the old violent beloved U.S.A." (I believe I'm still living through them.) I grew up in Detroit and was a teenager in the summer of 1967, when the inner city's bottled rage exploded, leaving whole blocks burned to ash and forty-three people dead. I was bewitched by Truman Capote's "nonfiction novel," *In Cold Blood*, a psychological portrait of two Breivik- and Rock-like nobodies who slaughtered a family in rural Kansas. The summer of Rock's rampage was also the Summer of Sam, when David Berkowitz was finally arrested after murdering six people and setting New York City on edge for more than a year. The Manson family murders were still fresh in the national memory. So mass violence and its companion, dread, were nothing new, and I understood that they were not confined to big cities like New York or small towns like Holcomb, Kansas, or Chambersburg, Pennsylvania. They dwell everywhere, at all times.

I'm also aware that in the four decades since I was a cub reporter in Chambersburg, the scale of the violence has been ratcheting up relentlessly, becoming more rococo and heartless. The ubiquity of guns in America is surely a contributing factor, but that's another argument for another day. In the aftermath of the latest mass killing—nine shot dead at an Oregon community college—today's edition of *The New York Times* has a front-page story stating that one reason it's difficult to prevent mass killers is because so many non-violent people fit the conventional profile of a mass killer. Gary Lee Rock certainly fit the profile, as spelled out by the Northeastern University criminologist James Alan Fox: "They have a history of frustration. They externalize blame. Nothing is ever their fault. They blame other people even if other people aren't to blame. They see themselves as good guys mistreated by others." Jeffrey Swanson, a professor at Duke University, added that mass killers often feel they do not belong, yet frequently live in "smaller town settings where belonging really matters."

By today's standards, the body count in Oregon was not particularly remarkable. It was eclipsed by the mass shootings at Virginia Tech (thirty-three dead); Newtown, Connecticut (twenty-seven dead); Columbine, Colorado (fifteen dead); Aurora, Colorado (twelve dead); Charleston, South Carolina (nine dead); and, most recently, Orlando, Florida (fifty dead). Then there was the wholesale slaughter in Waco (eighty-six dead); Oklahoma City (168 dead); and on 9/11 (2,966 dead and more than 6,000 wounded). As Knausgaard pointed out, Breivik and his crime have become "normalized." By today's standards, Gary Lee Rock's shooting spree would barely be considered news. Another way to say this is that in America today, everything is Twin Peaks.

Now comes the strange part. This inflation of violence doesn't trivialize what happened in Chambersburg in the '70s. Instead, it serves as a reminder that all human experience must be seen through the prism of its time and place. And for a cub reporter on a small-town daily in the '70s, the things I lived through were overwhelming. On bad days they pushed me all the way to the edge.

GARY LEE ROCK'S ACTS might be inexplicable, but the reporter in me needed to hear his version of what happened. Though I guessed it was hoping for too much, I wanted to see if I could get him to explain why he did what he did. So in 2012, while researching this book, I wrote a letter to Rock—inmate #AK5491—and mailed it to him at Huntingdon State Prison, the grim nineteenth-century fortress where he's serving a life sentence without possibility of parole. Rock did not reply to my letter, even to tell me he was not interested in being interviewed. I figured that was the end of it.

In the summer of 2014, I heard from Brad Bumsted, who was then working in Harrisburg as a reporter and columnist for *The Pittsburgh Tribune-Review*. Brad told me he'd just received an e-mail from a retired Chambersburg pastor named Ken Gibble, who described himself as a "frequent visitor" to Huntingdon State Prison and a "personal friend" of Gary Lee Rock's. After noting that Rock had published a pamphlet called *The Prisoners' Rights Handbook* in 2009, Gibble was writing to Brad to see if the *Tribune-Review* would print a new opinion essay Rock had written. In this new essay, "The Shawshank Redemption: What a 20-Year Old Film Can Teach Pennsylvania and Other States About Criminal Justice," Rock argues, counterintuitively but persuasively, that the rehabilitation function of the state's prison system, including the Parole Board, is a sham and a waste of tax dollars. "Hearing all this from (I'm ashamed to say it) a convicted murderer who has spend (sic) 37 years behind bars is no doubt upsetting to many," Rock's essay concludes. "One can hope that most taxpayers will disregard the messenger and focus on the message."

Intrigued, I called Ken Gibble and told him about my book project. Gibble agreed to see me, and so on my way to Chambersburg to do research in the spring of 2015, I stopped at Gibble's home in Camp Hill, not far from the prison where Rock had tried to commit suicide on the Fourth of July, 1977.

Gibble, an affable man, served me a cup of coffee and ushered me into his living room, where I noticed a book-marked copy of Anthony Trollope's novel, *The Warden*, on a table. As we talked, it occurred to me that this fastidious, upright man would have fit right in with the small-town clerics in a Trollope novel. From 1995 to 2001, Gibble told me, he served as pastor of the Church of the Brethren in Chambersburg, where the Rock family were long-standing members. Gibble, a native of Lancaster County, knew nothing about Gary Lee Rock or his crimes when he arrived in Chambersburg, but eventually the whispers reached him, and he wound up becoming Rock's "spiritual advisor," which each inmate is entitled to under Department of Corrections policy. Gibble started making regular trips to Huntingdon, at least twice a year, sometimes more often.

I asked Gibble if he and Rock spend much time talking about the events of the Fourth of July weekend in 1977. "The first time I visited Gary," Gibble replied, "I asked him if he wanted to talk about it. He said, 'All I want to say is that I did a terrible thing.' We kind of talk around it sometimes. Once he said to me, 'When you're young you do stupid things, and I did a stupid thing.'" Instead of dwelling on the crimes, Gibble said, they talk about books, sports, politics, prison life. Rock, according to Gibble, is an avid reader.

Gibble told me he was getting ready to visit Huntingdon, and I asked him if he would mention my book project and ask Rock if he would be willing to have me visit him at the prison. Gibble promised he would.

A month later I got an e-mail from Gibble. It read: "I've just returned from a visit with Gary this morning. I told him about your contact with me, explained that you are working on a book that would include events that occurred back in the '70s in the Chambersburg area, including his crime. I relayed the question you asked me to raise with him . . . would he consent to have you visit him? He responded with an emphatic 'No.' He did mention receiving the letter you sent him and told me that he intentionally did not write back. It's my opinion that he has no desire to revisit the events related to his crime."

I called Gibble to thank him for his trouble, then I gave up hope of ever interviewing Rock. His acts may or may not be inexplicable, but it was time to accept the likelihood that they will never be satisfactorily explained, by Rock or anyone else.

Mrs. Nibble

So the novice Tim O. Rockwell would be going up against a seven-term incumbent in the Democratic primary for the 90th District seat in the state House of Representatives. But William O. "Bill" Shuman was more than a political institution. He was an avatar, the living embodiment of the values and worldview of the people he represented in the most conservative swath of one of the most conservative counties in the state. No one knew that Shuman had just over a year to live. And no one could have imagined the spectacular way in which he would die.

Balding, bespectacled, and built like a bowling ball, Bill Shuman was born in Antrim Township, near Greencastle. He grew up poor. After working as editor and business manager at *The Greencastle Echo-Pilot* weekly newspaper, then as country treasurer, he got elected to the state House of Representatives in 1964. He never left. He was a born politician, a glad-hander and back-slapper, an assiduous presser of the flesh who had a boundless appetite for teaching Sunday school at the First United Methodist Church in Greencastle, for the parades, beauty pageants, graduations, funerals, bloodmobile drives, county fairs, service organization luncheons, and other stations of the cross that make up the life of a state-level politician. Shuman actually seemed to relish these endless duties at the altars of God, flag, and family. He prided himself on his "constituent service," which frequently amounted to expediting a driver's license renewal or helping unravel some other prosaic bit of red tape. He saw himself, not inaccurately, as a public servant.

A statesman he was not. Even a largely laudatory editorial in *Public Opinion* described him as "unctuous" and admitted that "he cut no great figure in the legislative halls of Harrisburg." But the people of southern Franklin County didn't want a great figure representing them in Harrisburg; they wanted one of their own, a solid, unpretentious, upstanding, God-fearing Christian. And that's precisely what they appeared to get in Bill Shuman. One characteristic piece of legislation he sponsored was a 1973 bill requiring all able-bodied persons receiving public assistance to work at local jobs. Even more than shirkers, Shuman hated taxes, especially the state's 6 percent sales tax, and he worked unsuccessfully to get certain items exempted from it, including ice cream bought at roadside stands. A decorated World War II veteran, he helped get Veterans Day returned from the fourth Monday in November to November 11, the original Armistice Day, which honored veterans of the First World War. It was a signal achievement.

Though Shuman was a knee-jerk opponent of tax increases and government spending, he didn't seem to mind that Pennsylvania's state legislators were (and still are) among the highest paid in the nation. "What made him popular," said a Democratic party operative, "was that he only voted one time for a tax." According to a published report, "Shuman was known for voting to implement state programs but not for the funds to pay for them." Indeed, at his press conference at the Mercersburg Inn announcing his candidacy, Tim Rockwell had chided Shuman for this politically expedient legerdemain. "I think if people want quality education and quality services, they're going to have to pay for them," Rockwell said. "I think it's outrageous to say you're going to increase subsidies without increasing taxes."

Brad Bumsted will never forget the first time he met Shuman, back when Brad was *Public Opinion*'s one-man Greencastle bureau. "I'm in the office," Brad recalls, "and this guy comes in and grabs my hand—this was his m.o.—and starts pumping it up and down like a jackhammer. He was strong, and he was crushing my hand. I'm thinking, who is this weirdo?"

My first encounter with Shuman came on the night I got sent out to cover one of his regular town hall meetings somewhere in Greencastle, a staple of his "constituent service" repertoire. On my way to the meeting I drove past a local landmark on US 11 south, the Gibble's potato chip factory, with the catchy "Nibble With Gibble's" logo on the big sign out front.

After Shuman's garbled remarks that night, I was in a panic. How could I possibly turn such gibberish into coherent English prose? When Shuman opened the floor to questions, a woman raised her hand. It was Mary Gibble, the potato chip doyenne, who started selling her irresistible chips at a farmer's market in the 1950s and had since built a thriving little empire. Shuman lit up at the sight of such a noteworthy constituent. He pointed to her and said, "Yes, Mrs. Nibble?"

The room erupted in laughter, and I couldn't help but join in—Mrs. *Nibble*, the guy's too much!—but as I studied Shuman's face I could see that he was mystified by the uproar. This, I realized, was not some glib pol making a clever joke. This guy wasn't even aware that he'd made a gaffe. That's how clueless Bill Shuman was.

Years later, when I heard the journalist Molly Ivins's quip—"The Texas state legislature will soon be in session, God forbid, leaving many a village without its idiot."—I immediately thought of the pride of Green-castle, Pennsylvania: William O. "Bill" Shuman.

We reporters weren't the only ones who regarded him as a laughingstock. During legislative sessions in Harrisburg, Shuman's fellow solons took turns shooting rubber bands at his shiny skull, a little bit of junior high school right there under the majestic green dome of the state capitol. Your tax dollars at work.

Shuman was a bachelor, he lived with his widow sister, he was active in the Boy Scouts—red flags all around—and there were persistent rumors that he was gay. "It was the worst-kept secret," Bob Vucic, then a reporter with *The Hagerstown Morning Herald*, recalled recently. "Everyone knew, but no one was willing to go on the record. In that sense, it was a little bit like the Jerry Sandusky story."

Gay or straight, the politically savvy Bill Shuman had the good sense to tell voters fantasies they wanted to hear, while the politically naïve Tim Rockwell thought it was his duty to tell voters realities they needed to hear. Even then, nearly a year before the primary, I could see that Tim Rockwell didn't have a chance of unhorsing Bill Shuman.

TURNS OUT I MISSED my calling. I should have been a political consultant, or at least a pundit. In the Democratic primary the following May, Shuman demolished Rockwell by a 2-to-1 margin. But Shuman never got a chance to face off against the Republican challenger, Terry Punt, in the November election.

On August 30, 1978, while taking a rare vacation in Miami, Shuman collapsed from an apparent heart attack and was taken by ambulance to the University of Miami's Jackson Memorial Hospital, where he was pronounced dead on arrival. He was fifty-seven. The next day's news reports, in both the *Morning Herald* and *Public Opinion*, were short, factual recitations of the circumstances of Shuman's death, his early years, and his political career. "Exactly where and when Shuman was stricken remained unclear late Wednesday," the *Morning Herald* reported. "But based on information from rescue dispatchers, he was believed to have been transported from the intersection of Coral Way and 29th Avenue."

The *Public Opinion* reporters assigned to the story, Marty Rolfe and Dawn DeCwikiel-Kane, had all morning to do legwork, and they turned up an intriguing new detail: "The 57-year-old legislator was stricken while in the process of taking a shower at the Club Miami, a Miami health club, according to an unconfirmed report issued by the City of Miami Police Department."

The story was about to get steamy. The next day, the *Morning Herald* ran a screamer headline across the top of the front page:

"REP. WILLIAM SHUMAN DIED IN GAY BATHHOUSE IN MIAMI"

The article, written by Herb Perone, opened with the fact that Shuman was "using the facilities of the Club Miami, a well-known gay bathhouse," when he suffered his fatal heart attack. It continued, "According to Miami City Police reports, Shuman was coming out of the private club's steam room, clad in a towel, when he collapsed." Citing a Miami *Herald* story, Perone reported that the Club Miami's amenities included "a sunken sauna bath, approximately 40 four-foot-by-six-foot rooms equipped with beds, and a large room with mirrors totally covering the walls and ceiling and with a king-sized round bed in the middle. Scattered through the club was a collection of whips, chains and handcuffs. . . . There was also a television room where sex films could be viewed."

Dawn DeCwikiel-Kane was driving to work that morning when she heard the news on her car radio. She nearly drove off the road. She had heard the whispers, but she was not prepared for this. "There were rumors that Shuman was gay," she says, "and he certainly exhibited signs. But dying in a gay bathhouse is, as they say, a whole 'nuther story. What a way to come out!"

Indeed. Coming out while checking out.

"When I got to work," Dawn continues, "I recall that a few of us were kind of in shock at the irony of the whole thing. So I did reporting and learned what I could, because now I had specific questions to ask. But I think the reason we didn't lead with the gay bathhouse angle was because the *Morning Herald* had already broken the story, and we were sort of a second-day lede on it since we published in the afternoon. So we—I—didn't want to copy exactly what the *Herald* had done."

Dawn's story in that day's paper ran under an aggressively neutral headline—"Shuman's body being returned home"—and the scene of Shuman's death wasn't mentioned until the fourth paragraph: "Shuman collapsed Wednesday about 9 p.m. at the Club Miami, a well-known Miami gay health spa. He had taken a shower and was walking from the spa's steam room to the whirlpool when he collapsed." The story added that Shuman was a member of the private club and that membership was limited to males.

I asked Dawn if she was under pressure to tone down the story.

"It's possible that we toned it down a bit," she replied, "but my main feeling was that I didn't get the scoop and I didn't want to copy or steal from the competition. I don't recall being under any particular pressure to tone down the story."

Katy Hamilton has a slightly different memory of events. "With that kind of wild story, the reporter, editor and publisher discuss it," she says. "We had meetings before that story ran. You have to remember where Bill Shuman came from and who he represented. Franklin County is a very conservative area, and he was a very respected guy. We had the fact that he was gay in the story, but quite frankly I don't think our readers would have appreciated those kinds of gory details [which were in the *Morning Herald* story]. We wanted to inform, but we were never out for the gory details. If you have a business, any kind of business, you have to know your audience or clientele. Our audience doesn't like us to overdo it."

The story would have one last delicious twist. *Public Opinion*'s understated news coverage and a benign editorial about Shuman inspired just one letter to the editor. It was written by Charles E. Neubaum, Assistant State Adjutant of the American Legion, who praised the "fine" editorial and recalled Shuman's dedication to the American Legion and his work on getting Veterans Day returned to November 11. Neubaum's letter made no mention of the Club Miami.

Readers of the *Morning Herald*, on the other hand, bombarded the paper with outraged letters to the editor. One reader railed against the paper's "vicious innuendo and irresponsible journalism." Another wrote: "You deliberately reached for and achieved a new low in the brutal exploitation of human frailty . . . The *Morning Herald* crassly besmirched a dead man's memory with generalizations as to where he died and suggestive innuendos as to what brought him there." Other readers described the paper's coverage as "very cruel," "cheap shot," "shabby," and "journalism at its worst." My personal favorite came from Janet P. Miller of Greencastle: "You could learn a lesson from Chambersburg's *Public Opinion* of the same date. They used the word gay but in the fine print."

So it turned out that Katy Hamilton understood *Public Opinion*'s readership at least as well as Bill Shuman understood his constituency. The editor and the politician both understood that the human appetite for the truth has its limits, and sometimes it's wise to tell people what they want to hear. And if you absolutely have to reveal a distasteful truth, have the decency to do it *in the fine print.* At the very least, this will limit subscription cancellations and angry letters to the editor of the newspaper; and for the politician, it will enhance his chances of getting re-elected and, perhaps more important, of getting remembered in a rosy light.

More than one thousand people filed past Bill Shuman's open casket at the Minnich-Miller Funeral Home in Greencastle, and nearly five hundred people packed the First United Methodist Church the next day for his funeral. Reverend Glen A. Miller eulogized Shuman as a "tireless and energetic" legislator, which no one could fairly dispute. The *Morning Herald*, possibly chastened by the reader backlash, said only that Shuman "died of a heart attack while visiting Miami."

The *Herald*'s story concluded with this description of the scene at the graveside in Cedar Hill Cemetery, a sentence Ernest Hemingway might have written: "As light rain began to fall, two buglers played taps and a gun salute was fired."

The Nadir of the Glorious Nadir

The heat was brutal all summer long, and not only in central Pennsylvania. A mass of hot air blanketed the country, radiating outward from a molten core shaped like a distended eggplant stretching from Texas to Minnesota. The Eastern Seaboard was an oven. Something had to give, and it did, spectacularly, on July 13, when lightning struck New York City's over-worked electric grid and the lights started winking out. Power remained out for the next twenty-five hours, inspiring an orgy of looting and arson throughout the city. There were 1,000 fires and 3,700 arrests. Looters were especially industrious on Brooklyn's Broadway, where electronics stores were preferred targets. The sound quality of the nascent hip-hop movement enjoyed a major upgrade after the summer of '77, thanks to the abundant five-finger discounts on microphones, speakers, mixing boards, and other goodies during the blackout.

A twenty-year-old woman from Seattle, identified only as Keelin, was living in Brooklyn that summer, and years later she spun this riff for *The New York Times*:

> What with the heat, the fire hydrants fanning out big sprays across the streets full of sweaty people, the looting, no subways, little work, no elevators, no refrigerators, Son of Sam

roaming around, boyfriend sick, and punk rock as sound track in my head, Blackout '77 was a surreal, fun, scary holiday in New York City during its glorious nadir.

The glorious nadir—what an apt way to describe the '70s! (Another apt description comes from the British writer Martin Amis, who called it "the joke decade.") For me, this glorious nadir of a decade had a distinct beginning, a distinct nadir, and a distinct end. The beginning was September 9, 1971, the morning a classmate and I set out from my parents' home in Syracuse to hitchhike to Providence for the start of our sophomore year of college. We stood on the shoulder of an on-ramp to the eastbound New York State Thruway, thumbs out, RHODE ISLAND Magic Markered on a scrap of cardboard, a couple of longhairs who couldn't buy a ride.

When we finally got a lift, we looked across the grassy median at an astonishing sight. In the passing lane on the opposite side of the Thruway, dozens of carloads of state troopers were heading west at high speed, bumper to bumper, flashers blazing, and sirens screaming.

"Something big must be happening," the driver remarked.

"Yeah," my stoner buddy nodded. "They're probably trying to get to Dunkin' Donuts before it closes."

Not quite. The troopers were headed to Attica State Prison, 125 miles to the west, where some 1,000 prisoners had rioted and taken three dozen staff members hostage that morning. After barricading themselves into a cellblock, the prisoners produced a list of demands, including better medical treatment and an end to brutal treatment by guards. A team of negotiators was brought in, including Tom Wicker of *The New York Times* and Louis Farrakhan of the Nation of Islam. After several days of tense talks, a peaceful resolution to the crisis appeared within reach. But Governor Nelson Rockefeller refused to go to the prison to meet the inmates, and he rejected their demands for total amnesty and removal of the prison superintendent. Instead, with Rockefeller's blessing, state troopers and National Guardsmen stormed the prison on September 13, firing more than 2,000 rounds of ammunition. When the tear gas cleared and the guns fell silent, forty-three people lay dead— thirty-three inmates and ten corrections officers and civilian employees. Police then beat and tortured scores of prisoners.

Up to that point, it was the bloodiest single day in American history since the Civil War. Though a subsequent investigation would show that the bloodshed was both avoidable and unnecessary—a "turkey shoot," in the words of one Rockefeller critic—President Richard Nixon telephoned the governor to congratulate him. Nixon had campaigned for the presidency in 1968 on a platform of "law and order"—a thinly veiled promise to get tough with drug dealers and the students and inner-city (that is, black) residents who had spent the '60s protesting too much for Nixon's taste. On the telephone the day of the Attica raid, Nixon told Rockefeller, "But the courage you showed and the judgment in not granting amnesty, it was right, and I don't care what the hell the papers or anyone else says." Nixon went on to describe the rebellion, inaccurately, as "basically a black thing." Rockefeller then misreported the extent of the shooting and bloodshed, concluding, "It really was a beautiful operation . . . this separated the sheep from the goats."

As with any artificial marking of time, there are many ways to claim when one decade ended and the next one began. Soon after Nixon got elected in 1968, the Manson family went on its helter-skelter spree, the Altamont rock festival ended in murder, National Guardsmen shot four anti-war protesters dead at Kent

State University in Ohio, and Jack Kerouac died drunk. Did any or all of those events mark the end of the '60s? Not for me, not quite. In the spring of 1970, a month before my high school graduation, I saw my first Grateful Dead concert at the Fillmore East in New York City, but even then I could sense that the '60s were over and I'd pretty much missed the party. Then the Attica bloodbath confirmed it. Rockefeller completed his separation of the sheep and the goats by passing the Draconian sentencing laws that bear his name, sending thousands of minor criminals to long prison stretches. The nation still hasn't recovered. Law and order, indeed. How telling that Donald Trump dusted off Nixon's buzzwords during his own successful campaign for the presidency.

Keelin's mention of the punk rock soundtrack during the '77 New York blackout reminded me of the many things I missed out on when I willingly entered that backwoods monastery for workaholics known as the *Public Opinion* newsroom. I'd checked out of pop culture long before then, even before I was force-fed a steady diet of Peter Frampton's talking guitar at the Record Bar. I'd begun checking out after the Attica prison riot, during the ensuing rise of disco and Elton John, the Bee Gees, and Wings. Paul McCartney used to be in the Beatles, for chrissakes, and now he was singing "Silly Little Love Songs"? Then, a year before the decade's nadir, I ran up against the band that broke my back: Fleetwood Mac.

For my final semester of college, in early 1976, I moved into the vacant bedroom in an off-campus apartment occupied by a fish out of water named Rick von Schweinitz. Rick was a blue-collar kid from Coos Bay, Oregon, who'd spent his boyhood summers working aboard his father's tuna boat, trolling up and down the Pacific Coast slathered in fish guts and blood. With a workingman's calloused hands, permanently curled fingers, and thick wrists, Rick did not look like typical

Ivy League material, which was one of the many things I liked about him. I'd cut off my hair by then—the '60s were ancient history—and though Rick still wore his in a long ponytail, he was less of a hippie than I was. I was still an equal-opportunity drug user, but the only drug Rick ever did was Budweiser, which he drank by the case. And his absolute #1 most favorite album in the history of the universe was the eponymous *Fleetwood Mac*, which he played, more or less, all the time.

The band was everything I detested about the '70s: slick, self-indulgent, pseudo-profound. So I stayed in my bedroom with the door closed, flying on speed, typing like a banshee to finish my history of Providence in time for graduation. If I didn't complete the book, I wouldn't have enough credits to graduate. As a cure for writer's block, this was way more effective than the deadline on a daily newspaper. Hour after hour I tried to blot out Stevie Nicks whining "Rhe-*aaaaaaaaaaaaaaaa-non*" and:

> *Cause when the lovin' starts and the lights go down,*
> *There's not another livin' soul around.*
> *You woo me un-til the sun comes up*
> *And you saaaaaaaaay-ay that you love me.*

To this day, a few bars of Fleetwood Mac or Elton John or Peter Frampton teleport me straight back to the '70s. But now, from a distance of many years, I've begun to see that the decade wasn't pure cheese. Keelin's riff about the punk rock soundtrack during the blackout led me indirectly to Will Hermes's book *Love Goes to Buildings On Fire*, which reminded me just how much great new music I missed at the time—the New York Dolls, Television, Tuff Darts, Willy DeVille, Patti Smith, the Ramones. Such stuff rarely penetrated the walls of our backwoods monastery. Then, in *Please Kill Me: The*

Uncensored Oral History of Punk, Joey Ramone spoke directly to my Fleetwood Mac problem:

> We did (our first) album in a week and we only spent sixty-four hundred dollars making it – everybody was amazed. At that time people did not have that much regard for money. There was a lotta money around. Money circulating for absurd things. Money wasn't tight yet – some albums were costing a half-million dollars to make and taking two or three years to record, like Fleetwood Mac and stuff.

The Fleetwood Mac album he was referring to was 1977's *Rumours*, which Sam Anderson, writing in *The New York Times*, would call "an exquisitely engineered soft-rock juggernaut that went platinum 20 times over, spent 31 weeks at #1 and made Fleetwood Mac the world's biggest band." Such success did what it usually does—it puffed up the egos, turned the hillocks of cocaine into Himalayas, and led to unfettered self-indulgence. Fleetwood Mac's next album, *Tusk*, took more than a year to record at a cost of more than $1 million, making it the most expensive record ever made at the time. Even so, it flopped, selling one-tenth as many copies as *Rumours*. But one band's dud is another critic's under-appreciated masterpiece, and Anderson gave the album a pass: "It is where obsessive artistic control circles around into raggedness, where chaos and order dance together in a cloud of swirling scarves. The album has probably five too many songs, and a handful of tracks are two minutes too long, but that's the cost of this kind of genius: excess, bombast, hubris, getting carried away."

Though this was intended as high praise, I haven't read a more deft skewering of everything I loathed about the '70s.

THE NADIR OF THE GLORIOUS nadir, both in my life and in the life of the nation, was the summer of '77. My summer of Gary Lee Rock was New York's summer of Sam. The summer of my mother's death was the summer of the surreal, fun, scary holiday of the New York blackout. The season when Fleetwood Mac reached its zenith was the season when the South Bronx was ablaze during the World Series, the parallels to Nero's Rome impossible to miss. The country was grinding through the worst economic times since the 1930s, a time of oil shocks, high unemployment and high inflation, the dismal end of a lost war, all of it overseen by three failed presidencies. New York in those days was even hairier than Baltimore. Among the decade's many brilliant, auteur-driven movies, few captured the menace and rot of the city's streets better than *The French Connection* or *Taxi Driver*. The place fascinated me even as it scared the piss out of me, a scorched shell full of dangerous shadows and deep-pore grime.

"New York felt empty—there were so many parts of it where people didn't want to go—and out of control," the critic and author Louis Menand wrote recently in *The New Yorker*. "It was the time of broken windows. But, in part because of the collapse, the city also felt open, liberated, available. Anything seemed possible. . . ."

Those words were contained in a review of Garth Risk Hallberg's staggeringly ambitious—and staggeringly good—911-page debut novel, *City on Fire*. The novel culminates on July 13, 1977, the night of a thousand arson fires, and as Menand suggests, it's a portrait of how the fires and the abandonment and the crime and the grime were actually liberating for people of a certain temperament. Keelin knew this. Will Hermes and Joey Ramone knew this. Garth Risk Hallberg knows this. And so does Dan Epstein, a writer I bumped into in a bar called Nemo's in Detroit in the summer of 2014, while we were on our separate book tours. Dan gave me a copy of his delirious take on '70s baseball, *Big Hair and Plastic Grass: A Funky Ride Through Baseball and America in the Swinging '70s*, and as I read it I realized he reveled in the cheesiness of the '70s—not only the era's baseball, but its fashions and its politics and especially its music—and he did it without the killing smirk of irony. And he had the big hair and the muttonchops to prove it. What's not to love, Dan asks, about the decade that gave us the Detroit Tigers' loopy pitcher Mark "The Bird" Fidrych and Pittsburgh's Dock Ellis, the only pitcher ever to throw a no-hitter while zonked on LSD?

Because of these and other colorful characters, baseball in the '70s, Dan writes, "exuded an edgy (and palpably exciting) anything-goes vibe, one that has long vanished from the game as we know it. In recent years, for example, the Atlanta Braves have held a 'Faith Day' promotion, featuring performances by Christian rock bands and testimonials from Braves players about how Jesus turned their lives around. This is the same team that, back in 1977, drew more than 27,000 fans for a 'Wet T-Shirt Night' competition. Give me the 1970s any day."

Point taken. Just as my '54 Buick had given me a way to question easy assumptions about the '50s as a time of bland Eisenhower conformity, Keelin and Will Hermes and Garth Risk Hallberg and Dan Epstein had given me a way to question my memories of the '70s as a time of 100 percent homogenized cheesiness. In the *Doonesbury* comic strip, Zonker Harris dubbed the '70s "a kidney stone of a decade." Maybe so, but amid the cheese and the kidney stones there was a staticy vibe, a disconnect, a dissonance that has proven strangely alluring. The times were anything but homogeneous; they were cracked, crazed, schizo. For some writers—myself included, as it turns out—bad times can be the best times. And everything about the '70s was bad in a good, jagged way. It was a time of gay rights and women's rights and prisoners' rights and "law and order" and the Rockefeller laws. It was a time of soft rock and disco, with funk and punk and hip-hop bubbling up through the cracks in the sidewalk. It was the time of the first Earth Day and the opening of the trans-Alaska pipeline. You could see the Ramones for a dollar at C.B.G.B.'s downtown or watch Bianca Jagger ride a white horse onto the dance floor at Studio 54 uptown. It was when people scrambled to get on board the last helicopter to leave a Saigon rooftop, and more than 900 people drank the Kool-Aid in Jonestown. It was a time of peace talks in Paris and bombings at home, more than 1,900 domestic bombings in 1972 alone, the targets ranging from the US Capitol to a popular Wall Street lunch spot. You needed a program to keep track of the alphabet soup of pissed-off posses working to hasten the imminent overthrow of the US government—the SLA, the BLA, FALN, NWLF, the Weather Underground, the Family, even the Jewish Defense League—an unhinged army of bombers, kidnappers, bank robbers, trust funders, and stone-cold killers. Criminals ranged from diabolical to goofy to mystifying and back again: Charles Manson, Patty Hearst, Gary Lee Rock, Gary Gilmore, the Son of Sam.

That domestic bombing spree figured prominently in Philip Roth's Pulitzer Prize-winning novel *American Pastoral*, which tells the story of a sensationally handsome and athletic Jewish boy from Newark named Seymour "Swede" Levov, who marries a former Miss New Jersey, takes over his father's thriving glove factory, and moves his wife and daughter into an old stone farmhouse out past the suburbs, way out in the gorgeous, green folds of the American pastoral. There, as a way of protesting the Vietnam War, Swede's daughter plants a bomb in the local post office that kills a respected doctor, forcing the girl to go underground and effectively demolishing Swede's pristine world. He has become, Roth writes, the victim of something unthinkable: "The daughter who transports him out of the longed-for American pastoral and into everything that is its antithesis and its enemy, into the fury, the violence, and the desperation of the counterpastoral – into the indigenous American berserk."

ON AUGUST 16, 1977, two months after my mother's death, Elvis Presley suffered a massive heart attack and pitched off the upstairs toilet in Graceland, his bowels fatally blocked by the constipation that is the lot of every junkie. Elvis was dead at forty-two, and while the world mourned, I barely noticed. It was too sad and too perfect. The scarf-tossing, white jump-suited Elvis *was* the schizo '70s: excess, bombast, hubris, getting carried away in that place where chaos and order dance together in a cloud of swirling scarves. And, for good measure, a sick parody of what had come before.

The glorious nadir had reached its absolutely perfect nadir.

Ben Fucking Bradlee

Finally, mercifully, the summer ran out of steam. One day shortly after the trees had started shedding their leaves, I walked up to Katy Hamilton's desk and handed her a list of the coming week's school board meetings. Then I told her I was taking the week off—with pay—because I had amassed way more than forty hours' worth of overtime and that was the deal Bob Collins made when he hired me. My memory may be faulty on this, but I seem to remember that Katy was speechless and the newsroom grew quiet as I told her what I was about to do. I don't believe any reporter had ever had the nerve to do it before.

The reason I needed some time off was that I had a little errand to run out of town. I must have been brimming with unmerited confidence, because I had asked my father for an outlandish favor. I asked if he would try to arrange a job interview for me with a guy he'd worked with as a reporter before I was born, the man who was now the most famous newspaperman in the world, *Washington Post* executive editor Ben Bradlee. Even though I had not yet logged a full year at *Public Opinion* and had no business trying to get a job at the *Post*, I figured it couldn't hurt to ask. The most outlandish thing is that my father made the call, and Bradlee agreed to see me.

I can date the interview with some certainty to an October afternoon in 1977. I remember waking up on a friend's sofa in DC and putting on my one suit, the same cheap pin-striped rig I'd worn to all those fruitless job interviews a year earlier. I had several hours to kill, so I ate a leisurely breakfast while giving the *Post* a close reading. Then, to stave off the jitters, I decided to take in a matinee showing of François Truffaut's new movie, *The Man Who Loved Women*, which had opened October 1 at the New York Film Festival.

The movie did its job—I was smitten by the lead character Bertrand, who is so smitten by so many women that it actually kills him in slapstick fashion. (It's a French movie.) Soon after leaving the theater I found myself riding an elevator to the fifth floor of the *Post* building and following a secretary across the eerily familiar newsroom that had played such an important role in the previous year's movie version of Bob Woodward and Carl Bernstein's *All the President's Men*. No sign of Robert Redford or Dustin Hoffman working the phones. Nixon's head wasn't mounted on any of the walls. I snapped out of it in time to realize that the man with the watered hair and expensive teeth waiting for me inside the glass-walled fishbowl office was not Jason Robards. It was, no doubt about it, Ben Bradlee.

After a gravelly "Hullo" and "Have a seat," his first words to me were, "Did your old man ever tell you if he fucked that hot redheaded waitress at People's Drug Store, Bernice Franklin?"

Delighted by the sight of my jaw hitting floor, obviously the desired effect, Bradlee launched into a story I knew only in vague outline. He and my father had worked together in the late 1940s on an exposé of a major DC gambling operation. Their main source was Bernice Franklin, "the prototypical waitress with a heart of gold and dyed red hair," as Bradlee would woodenly describe her in his 1995 memoir. Bernice was in love with a crippled newsstand operator named Till Acalotti, who took numbers and horse bets on the side. One night, as Bernice watched through the drugstore's windows, two detectives beat Till unconscious, apparently for failing to pay off the cops. So Bernice was singing about police complicity in the city's gambling rackets, and Bradlee and my father were writing down every word she warbled.

The *Post* in those days was hungry and poor, the #3 paper in a four-paper town. One of its primary targets was the district's chief of police, Robert Barrett, an old-school Southern segregationist who presided over a largely white, largely racist, and baroquely corrupt force. The *Post* brass was hoping that Bernice Franklin's inside knowledge would bring Barrett down. But while my father's and Bradlee's series was running on the front page, Bernice vanished mysteriously, and soon the rival *Times-Herald* riposted with its own banner headline: "Star Girl Witness About Faces, Unfolds New Version of Gaming Probe."

"Boy," my father recalled years later, "you'd have thought the top went off our building. Our editors wanted to know if Bradlee and I didn't have some of closer 'relationship' with Bernice Franklin. We said hell no, we didn't have anything more to do with her."

Eventually, FBI agents found Bernice, and she stuck with her original story, after admitting that the *Times-Herald* did "more" for her while all the *Post* had done was buy her a few dinners. Indictments came down, Barrett resigned under pressure, and the roof returned to the top of the *Post* building.

The success of the series made the city desk hungry for more. The managing editor, Russ Wiggins, paired my father with the *Post*'s veteran police reporter, Alfred E. Lewis, to write a series on the district's protected numbers kingpin. Their series, "The Charmed Life of Emmett Warring," ran on the front page every day for a week, with two full-page jumps inside. Those stories were near the top of the pile of crumbling clips in the footlocker I'd discovered in our attic in the early 1960s. As impressive to me as the clips was the carbon copy of a single-spaced, typed memo from Russ Wiggins to Al Lewis and my father. Wiggins spelled out, in microscopic detail, the sorts of things he wanted his reporters to dig up on Emmett Warring: the brand of booze he drank and how much of it; how many pairs of shoes he owned, how much they cost, and on and on. This was my first glimpse of the invisible editorial hand at work behind all good writing.

Bradlee, in his memoir, called my father "the fastest typist in the newspaper business," to which my father, a proud man, sniffed, "I like to think I was the fastest *writer* in the newspaper business." There's no disputing that he was lightning fast and a gifted rewrite man who could assemble a mass of reporters' phoned-in material and marshal it into crisp prose on a deadline.

As I'd learned at a young age, my father was also an exacting editor. During my junior year of high school, I came downstairs one night, terribly proud of myself, eager to show him my seventeen-page, typewritten paper on Albert Camus. I had not yet taken a course in touch-typing, so in addition to the reading and writing, this represented hours of hunt-and-peck torture. My father read the first sentence and frowned. I froze. He kept a matching gold-plated Cross pen and pencil set in his shirt pocket at all times, and to my horror, he took out the pen, not the pencil, and screwed out the ballpoint tip. With a flourish he circled a word, then recited my opening sentence: "By the time of his premature death in 1960 at the age of 46, Albert Camus had cemented his reputation as one of the major writers of the 20th century." My father looked over the top of the page and said, "The word *premature* refers to an early birth. If someone dies before it's expected, he suffers an *untimely* death." He proceeded to obliterate my masterpiece with blue ink cross-outs and editorial comments. Watching him work, I nearly wept. Then I spent the night re-writing and re-typing the paper, and of course I got an A-plus. Far more important, I'd learned two things that all writers need to know: that every unnecessary word must go; and if a word is wrong, it must be removed and replaced with the right word. And there is always a right word. Flaubert knew this a century ago, and now I knew it, too.

My father and Al Lewis made the perfect team. As my father put it, "Al was an old-time police reporter, a little short Jewish fella who knew all the cops in town, hung around police headquarters, and was always getting scoops on the competition. He was a very good reporter, but he couldn't write his name. So he'd get the information, and I'd write the stories."

Their "Charmed Life of Emmett Warring" series won the Page One Award from the Washington Newspaper Guild and was nominated for a Pulitzer Prize, though it failed to win. Al Lewis wound up working at the *Post* for fifty years, finally retiring in 1985. A dozen years before his retirement, on Sunday, June 18, 1972, the *Post* ran its first story about a bungled break-in at the Democratic National Committee headquarters in the posh Watergate complex. Eight reporters, including Bob Woodward and Carl Bernstein, contributed legwork to the story. It appeared under the headline "5 Held in Plot to Bug Democrats' Office Here." It was written by Alfred E. Lewis.

AS I SAT THERE in the glass fishbowl, Bradlee went on and on about what a hot fucking piece of ass Bernice Franklin was, what a bunch of racist pricks the DC cops were in those days, what a fucking peckerwood Robert Barrett was, what a great fucking shoe-leather reporter Al Lewis was. I've been around my share of salty tongues, but I have never heard anyone who could match the fluorescence and sheer pre-pubescent, potty-mouthed gusto of Ben Fucking Bradlee. At a journalism awards ceremony in 2008, Bob Woodward spoke about Bradlee's profanity:

> When Alan Pakula, who was the director for "All the President's Men," was assembling the cast, he and the actors decided that they wanted Jason Robards to play Bradlee. He said they would pay him $50,000, a lot of money for Jason Robards at this time, and they gave him the script. And Robards was delighted. He went home and read it, and then he came back to meet with Pakula and the actors and said, "I can't play this part. Have you read the script?" And they said, "Yes, we have, what's wrong?" And he said, "Ben Bradlee, all he does in the script is run around and say, 'Where's the fucking story?'" And they said to him, "What you're going to have to do is figure out fifteen ways to play that so it's different, so it's elegant," and that's actually what he did.
>
> The genius of Bradlee will never be reduced to a sentence or a paragraph, but it is: he understood that that's what the executive editor does. He runs around and finds different and elegant ways to say, "Where's the fucking story?"

Bradlee got a pass from a lot of people—subordinates, rivals, bosses, lovers—because, well, because he was Ben Bradlee. Because, among many other achievements, he conducted the orchestra that brought down the President of the United States and sent half of his staff to prison. But as I sat there listening to Bradlee's monolog, it occurred to me he had asked only glancingly after my father, and he had expressed zero interest in why I was sitting there in the fishbowl sharing his oxygen. I realized I was not participating in a job interview, I was witnessing a performance, but a complicated one. The performer had recently been played by an actor who had won an Oscar for his portrayal of the performer in a feature film that attempted to recreate historical events. The making of the movie version of Woodward and Bernstein's bestselling nonfiction book was a trip down a rabbit hole. It was, as Bradlee would later put it, "a strange new adventure into the fantasy world of actors playing real people in a fictional version of real history."

Meta enough for you? As I considered the performer's pedigree—Boston WASP, St. Mark's, Harvard, US Navy, the *Post*, Paris, *Newsweek*, hobnobbing with Jack and Jackie Kennedy, the Pentagon Papers, and then, most spectacularly, Watergate and its Hollywood echo chamber—it wasn't hard to see the motivation behind Bradlee's act. This Boston Brahmin wanted me—he wanted the world—to see him not as some silver-spoon pretty boy, but as a street-smart, salt-of-the-earth, wised-up, no-bullshit guy. Maybe he truly was all those things. But if so, I asked my twenty-five-year-old self, why is he working so hard to sell me on it? Why is he going after a gnat with a sledgehammer?

Years would pass before a possible answer came to me. In his 2012 book, *Yours in Truth: A Personal Portrait of Ben Bradlee*, Jeff Himmelman pointed out that when I met him in the fall of 1977, Bradlee had just come off an astonishing run—the *Post*'s Pulitzer Prize for its Watergate coverage in 1973, Nixon's resignation in 1974, the publication of Bradlee's memoir *Conversations With Kennedy* in 1975, and the heady premiere of the Oscar-winning *All the President's Men* in 1976. By the fall of 1977, according to Himmelman, there was a widespread feeling, both inside and outside the *Post* newsroom, that Bradlee was out of touch and the paper was drifting. One reporter said that Bradlee "was really out to lunch in the post-Watergate era." Bradlee received an unsigned, nine-page memo that included a prescient criticism of a flaw that would lead to catastrophe in a few years: "There are so many little things you don't know that are kept from you by your editors." The memo was written by Sally Quinn, a writer in the paper's "Style" section who would soon become Bradlee's third wife.

The post-Watergate hangover at the *Post* even became fodder for a *Doonesbury* comic strip. Way back in the fall of 1974, a strip about the "lost momentum problem" at the paper ends with an editor, obviously Bradlee, exhorting the newsroom troops: "C'mon, gang, let's get out there and get those great failing economy stories!!" This is greeted with a collective *"GROAN!!"*

As I sat there in the fishbowl listening to Bradlee's burbling river of profanity, it didn't occur to me that it was inspired by something as banal as boredom. In hindsight, it does make some sense. Eventually, the river ran dry. Maybe Bradlee got bored with listening to his own bullshit, because he sprang to his feet and ordered me to follow him.

As I trailed him across the movie-set newsroom, I could sense the crackle of electricity he gave off, reporters noticing his presence while making a point of pretending not to notice, curious eyes sizing me up, trying to figure out if I was a new copyboy or a potential rival. The point was that anyone who got inside Bradlee's office merited sizing up.

As it turned out, I was not the only one who felt the uncanniness of that newsroom, so familiar and yet so strange, a very real place that was also a memory, a fantasy, a prop. In his memoir Bradlee recalled paying a visit to the movie set of *All the President's Men*:

(Robert) Redford re-created the *Post* newsroom in incredible detail on a Burbank, California, lot . . . One morning [my daughter and I] walked onto the set together, and I was stunned. There were the same desks we had at the *Post*, the same colors, the same layout. The desks were covered with the same "dressing" – which had been swept off the tops of *Post* desks in Washington and shipped to California.

Now Bradlee stopped at the actual desk of an actual reporter who was easily the oldest person in the room. He was so old, he didn't even pretend to be hard at work on the paper's next Pulitzer. He gave me a quizzical look.

"Murrey," Bradlee said, "this is Dick Morris's kid, Bill, looking for a job." He turned to me. "Meet Murrey Marder. We both worked with your old man back in the day."

We shook hands. I recognized the name. My father loved to tell stories about his colorful *Post* colleagues, including Bradlee, Al Lewis, the publisher Phil Graham, the sportswriters Shirley Povich and Mo Siegel, the cartoonist Herblock, and the guy who covered Senator Joseph McCarthy and became the paper's diplomatic correspondent—Murrey Marder. My father said everyone called him Morey Murder. The man had a warm smile, and he asked after my father with far more interest than Bradlee had shown. As our brief conversation ended, I was relieved I didn't pull a Bill Shuman and call him "Mr. Murder."

I continued following Bradlee across the newsroom— the place seemed to go on forever—until we reached our destination, the office of city editor Leonard Downie Jr. Bradlee, possibly suffering from post-performance deflation, or possibly realizing he had actual work to do, made a quick hand-off. Then he was gone.

Downie was cordial and gave me more of his time than I deserved. He accepted my clips and résumé and promised to get in touch if anything opened up, which we both understood to mean that if I left his office and took two quick right turns, I would find the elevators.

WALKING UP 15TH STREET in the crisp autumn air, I felt a pair of mismatched emotions: disappointment tinged with relief. The disappointment wasn't hard to figure. I woke up that morning believing Ben Bradlee was a god, and now I knew for a fact that he was just another one of us mortals. His performance during my "job interview" was a disappointment not because of his laughable profanity or his lack of interest in my boundless potential but, rather, because of his overweening love for himself, or, more precisely, for his own myth. Of course it was possible Bradlee had acted like this long before Richard Nixon or Jason Robards came into his life. If so, the scenario was even grimmer, because many people have had their heads turned by fame and by Hollywood's reflected glow, and who can blame a mere mortal for that? On the other hand, if Bradlee had always been this full of himself . . .

But Bradlee's performance was just the beginning of a larger disappointment. My boyhood discovery of my father's clips in the footlocker, augmented by his stories about Bradlee and Al Lewis and Morey Murder, his stories about hanging out at the Atlas Club and other after-hours joints with newspapermen and bookies and mobsters, all conspired to make *The Washington Post* a magical place in my imagination, the ultimate place to work. This was not the cliché of a son yearning to walk in his father's footsteps; rather, it was a vague romantic belief that since my discovery of my father's writings had helped birth my dream of becoming a writer, it was only fitting that one day I would work where he had worked. And a job at the paper had become even more tantalizing to me in recent years, and not because of

Watergate, but because of the magnificent writing that was appearing every day in one of Bradlee's many innovations, the paper's "Style" section.

Then Watergate happened. Then the nation's history swamped my humble scrap of family history, along with the fantasy it had spawned. The *Post* was now much more than a desirable place to work. It was the Holy Grail, and not only for me, but for a whole generation of reporters. And this, curiously, was where the relief came in. Just as my articles about Dr. Robert Kochenour had taught me I had no interest in bagging big game, my encounter with Bradlee taught me I had no interest in going after the thing every reporter was expected to covet—a berth in the movie-set newsroom of *The Washington Post*. Yes, Bradlee's outsize ego was a turnoff, but the real questions became evident: do I want to be one of the hundreds of people sitting at a desk in that endless newsroom, always noticing the presence of the god with the watered hair and always pretending not to notice? Do I care, in turn, if he notices me? This was not stage fright or fear of failure or even the reporter's eternal dread of getting scooped. This was something much deeper. This was relief at being freed from a dream that had been programmed into me since boyhood, a dream that had once seemed personal but was now virtually universal. Bradlee had, inadvertently, made it possible for me to admit that the Holy Grail didn't matter to me. The writing was all that mattered to me, and this, in turn, reminded me of Marshall Frady's claim that small towns are particularly felicitous locations in which to set up in the business of writing novels. So are big cities, I now realized, and remote shacks, and submarines, and the suburbs. The point is that fine writing can be made out of absolutely anything, and it can be made to happen absolutely anywhere. So it was a tremendous relief to realize I did not have to want what I was supposed to want. I was free to pursue my dream in my own way, in my own places, in my own time.

But driving across Maryland in the gathering dusk, I could see that if Washington wasn't the place for me, neither was Chambersburg. I had outgrown the town and the job, and I needed to move on. So when I got home I started sending clips and résumés to papers where a reporter with a year's worth of experience had a realistic chance of getting offered a job. My apprenticeship was far from complete, but now it needed to go to the next level.

Leonard Downie Jr. never called, which didn't surprise me. Neither did any of the other editors who'd received my clips, which did surprise me. I was stuck. Another Pennsylvania winter was on its way, and once again it was a beauty.

Not Mine to Know

It hit me, finally, late one wintry night as I was driving home from covering yet another Tuscarora School Board meeting in Mercersburg. I was in the Buick heading northeast on Rte. 416, the same route I'd taken home after covering a Tuscarora School Board meeting my first night on the job. Thirteen years later, while working for a newspaper in North Carolina, I wrote a Mother's Day column about what happened that wintry night on my way home from Mercersburg:

> Strangely, the full force of her death didn't hit me until several months after the funeral. Death, I was to learn, can be a sneaky villain.
>
> I was driving home from a late-night newspaper assignment in rural Pennsylvania. I was cold and hungry and tired. I looked up at the black sky dusted with stars and suddenly I wanted to talk to her, to tell her what a long day it had been, how lost I felt, how frustrated I was in work and in love, the sorts of things only a mother ever truly understands. Not until that moment did I begin to fathom the black finality of her death. I had to pull off the road under those pulsing stars and cry until the realization had seeped into my bones, where it has dwelled ever since.

That detail about being "frustrated in love" may have been an embellishment, because I can't honestly recall if Maude and I were quarreling at the time. Then again, that column was written thirteen years after my mother's death, and another twenty-five have passed since it was written. So maybe after thirty-eight years I've forgotten something I recalled accurately after thirteen years. It's unlikely I'll ever know for sure.

But I am sure about the important details. It was a starry night, I'm sure of that, and I remember that on both sides of the road a stubble of corn stalks poked through the vast blankets of snow, blue in the moonlight. I remember windblown snow scurrying across the beam of my headlights. Why, it sounds like something out of a John Cheever short story, maybe "The Sorrows of Gin," which contains this description of a man driving home alone at night:

> He shivered with longing, he felt his skin coarsen as when, driving home late and alone, a shower of leaves on the wind crossed the beam of his headlights, liberating him for a second at the most from the literal symbols of his life—the buttonless shirts, the vouchers and bank statements, the order blanks, and the empty glasses. He seemed to listen—God knows for what.

So I pulled the Buick onto the shoulder of the road, and I wept. And as I wept I seemed to listen—God knows for what. I didn't hear any voices, and I didn't get any answers to any questions, asked or unasked, but I did come to a pair of important realizations. I understood, truly understood for the first time, that my mother was forever dead; and I understood that I needed to get away from this place, away from its insular people, its dreary winters, its rococo crimes, its dead teenage girls, its dead fire chiefs, its dead off-duty cops. There were too many ghosts at large in this small world, and now the ghost of my mother had joined them. Yes, I needed to get away from this place. At least, I consoled myself, I had taken a necessary, and healthy, first step into the cold realm of grief that night on the side of a snowy Pennsylvania back road.

My Mother's Day column addressed another aspect of my mother's death: my brother's unwillingness to reveal what he had seen, and how it had affected him, when he discovered our mother's lifeless body. I wrote:

> She was found on that bathroom floor by her first-born, my big brother, who hasn't been able to talk about that moment to this day. I understand, but I'm still waiting. I've often imagined he'll surprise me on a starry night by a mountain lake when we're old men and there's no longer any reason to keep our secrets or our sorrows to ourselves.

This, as it has turned out, was nothing more than wishful thinking and hollow poetry. Nearly forty years after our mother's death, I've stopped hoping that my brother and I will wind up together by a mountain lake, or that he'll ever reveal anything about our mother's death, to me, to himself, or to anyone else. It's obvious he doesn't have it in him, and that's something a man has to respect, even from his only brother, even from the one person who could reveal secrets and sorrows I once ached to know but have come to accept as unknowable. Or, at the very least, not mine to know. Which, in its way, is much, much worse.

"Al Neuharth Is a Snake."

By now it was apparent that all of us, including Bob Collins—no, *especially* Bob Collins—were working for the self-proclaimed sonofabitch who was the face of the Gannett corporation. Al Neuharth had been named CEO in 1973, two years after the company bought century-old *Public Opinion*, making it the twenty-seventh paper in the growing chain. Under Neuharth's whip, Gannett was now in its most robust phase of empire building, buying up the only newspaper in small and medium-sized towns, in essence building a string of monopolies that had a license to print money. It was a scorched-earth campaign that would soon make Gannett the largest and most profitable newspaper chain in the land, with added revenue coming from television and radio stations, plus the nation's largest outdoor advertising company. Neuharth's crowning glory, *USA Today*, was still in the larval phase, but already he had developed his imperial style and his reputation for being one ruthless sonofabitch.

Like most titans of industry, Al Neuharth was convinced that his performance—or, rather, Gannett's stellar performance on Wall Street—entitled him to the perks he so plainly relished. Even as he paid meager wages to the people toiling in the trenches of Gannett newsrooms, Neuharth dressed in designer clothes (always black and white), drank jumbo martinis and vintage bottles of Pouilly-Fuissé, traveled via Gulfstream jet and limousine, and kept suites at the Waldorf in New York and the Capital Hilton in Washington, DC. He also owned five houses, including an oceanfront compound in Cocoa Beach, Florida, near Cape Canaveral, the place that would soon become the launch pad of his most ambitious dream.

Brad Bumsted experienced the imperial Neuharth style first-hand shortly before I was hired at *Public Opinion*. Word went out in the newsroom one day that his majesty was coming to town for one of his dog-and-pony shows. The format never varied. The corporate jet would touch down at the nearest airport, in Hagerstown, Maryland, and a limo would ferry Neuharth to a hotel ballroom in Chambersburg, where local business leaders would be treated to a sumptuous spread and an Al Neuharth pep talk that was designed to quiet their grumbling about how Gannett's grand-larceny ad rates were hoovering their wallets. Of course the paper had to cover the show, a minefield of an assignment that reporters dreaded. Misquote Neuharth—or even fail to suggest that he walked on water—and you might as well start sending out résumés. Collins gave the delicate assignment to his most trusted reporter.

"It was nerve-wracking," Brad recalls. "I was sweating bullets, worried I might screw something up and be out of a job. Neuharth's this tough guy who doesn't fuck around. But in the end it was uneventful. I wrote the story and Collins went over it with a fine-toothed comb."

In the 1980s Brad would spend a few years working in the Gannett News Service bureau in Tallahassee, Florida, where Neuharth's second wife, Lori Wilson, served two terms as a state senator. Every year Neuharth threw one of his trademark bashes for the governor, legislative leaders, and corporate brass, and this time Brad didn't have to cover the event. He had to sit at the host's table, which may have been an even less enjoyable assignment.

"My bureau chief was almost like a caterer, making all the arrangements," Brad says. "Neuharth wanted to do it up right, and that party was a big deal." An ice sculpture on the buffet table was surrounded by mountains of shrimp, Apalachicola oysters, and crab legs. Top-shelf booze and fine wines flowed. The irony was not lost on Brad. "You see how cheaply Gannett papers had to survive, and here was this lavish feast for the corporate types," he says. "The gap between the have's and the have-not's was huge."

By way of making small talk that night, Brad mentioned to Neuharth that he would be making his first trip to New Orleans soon, then asked if there was anything special he should see. "He told me, 'You have to see it all,'" Brad says. "He was egotistical and arrogant. Pretty much what you'd expect from a sonofabitch."

AL NEUHARTH KNEW all about the have-not's of this world, and he wanted to have nothing to do with them. His biography puts Horatio Alger's in the shade. Neuharth was born poor in 1924 in Eureka, South Dakota, where his father ran a small creamery and died before the boy's second birthday. During the Depression, Neuharth's first job was collecting cow chips—sun-dried pancakes of manure—which people on the treeless prairie used as cooking fuel. Eventually, he graduated to delivering *The Minneapolis Tribune*, then to jobs as a butcher boy and soda jerk before working his way up to editor of the Alpena High School student newspaper.

After serving in the Army in World War II, Neuharth enrolled at the University of South Dakota and again rose to editor of the student newspaper. Then came reporting jobs with the *Associated Press* and Knight-Ridder's *Miami Herald,* which led to editing jobs in Miami and at *The Detroit Free Press.* In 1963 he jumped from Knight-Ridder to Gannett, a regional chain based in Rochester, New York, much smaller than Knight-Ridder. But Neuharth saw potential for growth. A decade later he was running the show, gobbling up newspapers, living like a maharaja. He'd come a long way from collecting cow chips in Bumfuck, South Dakota, and he had no intention of looking back.

I say Bob Collins *especially* was working for Al Neuharth, because Collins had hitched his star to the Gannett wagon at a young age, and it was the only company he'd ever worked for. Like Neuharth, Collins was a go-getter from humble origins with ambitions to climb the corporate ladder as high and far as it would take him. Like Neuharth, Collins was driven and demanding, sometimes ruthless, a self-made man who had gone to work in his father's Camden, New Jersey, luncheonette before he was tall enough to see over the counter. Collins's father gave him a pretzel can to stand on, and the boy would kick it along the floor and step up onto it to wait on customers. It was better than collecting cow chips, but not by much.

Collins worked at the luncheonette all through high school, sold Christmas trees and Easter flowers on the side, always hustling, always on the lookout for a new opportunity. In 1960, while still in high school, he got a job as a copyboy at *The Camden Courier-Post,* which Gannett had bought the previous year. Soon he was working as a night reporter in Plainfield, waiting tables and tending bar at a country club during the day, because he couldn't stand to be idle. By the time he met his future wife, Sue, at the Jersey Shore in 1968, Collins had begun his rise through the newsroom ranks, from reporter to night editor to Sunday editor. Gannett shipped him to Dickinson, North Dakota, then to Nyack, New York, then to *Public Opinion* as managing editor in 1974, the year after Neuharth became CEO. Two years later, shortly before he hired me, Collins was named president and publisher of the paper at the age of thirty-three, the youngest in company history. By then Collins was a certified Gannett golden boy, and it was obvious that Chambersburg was just a way station on his chosen path. The question was never if he would move on, but when.

In 1981, after quitting my third newspaper job, I drove the Buick up to the top of Maine, to the town of Ft. Kent, then turned around and drove south the length of old US 1, all the way to Key West, Florida. I interviewed people along the way and produced a nonfiction book that attempted to capture the zeitgeist of the country as seen through the wraparound windshield of a '54 Buick. President Dwight Eisenhower had unveiled his plan to build an interstate highway system the year my Buick rolled off the assembly line, and I thought a trip down an old pre-interstate road in my old Buick would be a novel way to take the nation's pulse. It was so novel that no publishers were interested.

US 1 passes through Camden, New Jersey, and I spent a night and a day there with Bob and Sue Collins. Bob's career had come full circle by then: he was president and publisher of the paper where he'd gone to work as a copyboy two decades earlier. After dinner at a Cherry Hills restaurant that night, I sat in the back seat of Bob's company car, a lime-sherbet and crabapple-green 1979 Pontiac Grand Prix with wire wheels, as he drove to their suburban home and he and Sue tried to explain why she had put together a string of five prize-winning Irish Setter show dogs. As I listened, I realized the story was not really about the dogs. It was about the climb up the Gannett corporate ladder, and the lot of the corporate wife.

"Well," Bob began, "one of the things I was noticing is that our marriage started off and I was a reporter and we had a boat, a 25-foot Owens. We went down to the shore and we'd have people down there and I had this job as a reporter. And people would ask about *my* boat and they'd talk about *my* job. I was noticing that people spent an awful lot of time asking about what I did and didn't ask Susan very much about what she did. At that time she was a housewife—and was very good at that— but I didn't think it made any sense. And so I said to Susan when we were transferred from North Dakota to Nyack that if we were to stay there, I thought one of the things we ought to do is get an Irish Setter puppy. If we did, then I would pay more for a show puppy if she promised to show it—thinking that at some point, if she became really good at it, when we got together with people they would be talking with Susan about the Irish Setters and what it is that she does."

He lit a fresh Merit cigarette, which he still chain-smoked the way he'd done during my job interview in Chambersburg five years earlier.

"And that's exactly what happened," he continued. "The day they told me I'd be staying on in Nyack, that night we went out and bought an Irish Setter show puppy. And Susan followed through on her commitment and started to show River. And I have made absolutely no attempt to know as much as Susan knows about Irish Setters, so that when we go to shows on Saturday and Sunday and I travel with her, people now talk to Susan about breeding and showing and all the things that dog people talk about. They hardly involve me in the conversation at all in terms of expertise. And I enjoy that very much."

"Yeah," Sue said, "at the dog shows he's Sue's husband. I'm not his wife."

"I'm not involved in the competition at all," Bob said, "but I share in her wins and I share in her losses and I'm as excited about her winning as she is. And that's really made a difference because what's happened here, Bill, is that Sue has had to give up a lot of things in terms of a constant lifestyle, of being in one area with friends and family. That's because of my job. The weekdays are mine; come the weekends they're very much Susan's and we do the kinds of things she wants to do. And almost every weekend that involves the dogs. It's really helped a lot."

We had arrived at the Collins' home, a sprawling five-bedroom Tudor-Mediterranean mash-up in the Shadow Lake development in the far suburb of Vincentown. The main reason they bought the house is the large backyard surrounded by a tall wooden fence, an ideal playpen for five high-strung Irish Setters. Bob and Sue had no children, so instead of baby pictures there were half a dozen pictures of Irish Setters on the walls of the foyer, the living room, and the den. The guest bedroom was decorated with an Irish Setter statuette and an Irish Setter wall clock.

While Bob took a phone call in the den, Sue introduced me to the dogs in the laundry room. They bumped against our legs, the washing machine, each other. Their tails whacked the walls, great white ropes of drool spinning from the corners of their mouths. When the mayhem got to be too much, Sue let the dogs gallop out into the backyard. "You really do go nuts with this," she said, shaking her head, smiling as she closed the door. "I don't even try to explain it to myself. I just do it."

Bob returned from the den and suggested we go out for a walk. It was past midnight, and Shadow Lake was asleep. Bob explained how Gannett handled changes in management personnel: word comes down from Rochester, the corporate jet arrives, and the manager is whisked to the next posting, sometimes under cover of darkness. Since it usually took less than twenty-four hours to move the pieces on the chessboard, Gannett managers were advised to keep a suitcase packed at all times. I asked Bob if he had ever considered turning down a promotion.

"That's not something that enters my mind," he said. "Quite simply, they've invested a lot of time and money in me, and at some point that has to be paid back. If they want me to go to Camden—fine. If they want to give me twelve hours' notice—that's okay, too. They know I'll do it. In many, many ways they've been good to me. I understand that the tradeoff is that when I'm needed, I'm expected to go. I think that's a fair tradeoff. If they called me right now and said, 'Start driving,' they know I'd do it."

AS I WAS RESEARCHING and writing this book, it occurred to me that I needed to read Al Neuharth's 1989 memoir, *Confessions of an S.O.B.* The book is a gleeful retelling of Neuharth's rise from Dakota rags to East Coast riches, sprinkled with boasts about out-maneuvering superiors, eavesdropping on rivals, manipulating colleagues, and ditching wives. It's written in the staccato Chinese-water-torture prose style Neuharth perfected in his column for *USA Today*, which debuted with great fanfare in 1982. It's the style of a deeply cynical writer who believes his readers are too dim or too lazy to hoist in grammatical sentences that convey complex ideas. Here, for instance, is Neuharth's description of Jimmy Hoffa: "Hoffa was the smartest tough man I've ever met. I've met smarter. A few tougher. But none as smart and as tough. He was a bad S.O.B." Praise from Al Neuharth did not get higher than this. To give his book some heft, he quotes many great thinkers, from Seneca to Zsa Zsa Gabor.

Neuharth's writing style goes a long way toward explaining what set *USA Today* apart from conventional American newspapers. Under Neuharth's orders, *USA Today* was full of bright graphics, color pictures, and short, upbeat articles that made cloying use of the first-person plural, as in this actual front-page headline: "Men, Women: We're Still Different." One *USA Today* editor conceded that the paper "brought new depth to the meaning of the word shallow." It also pioneered the dumbing-down that swept the American newspaper industry in the 1980s and '90s as it grappled with changing technologies, and shrinking readership and ad revenues. Many newspapers, with an assist from the Internet, dumbed themselves to death.

Reading Neuharth's book is the literary equivalent of eating cheese puffs: the more you consume, the less satisfied you feel. With each passing page I worried that I'd lost another point off my IQ, a loss I can scarcely afford. The book's lone indelible line comes from ex-wife #2, the former Florida state senator Lori Wilson: "Al Neuharth is a snake."

When I was about halfway through *Confessions of an S.O.B.*, another one of those non-coincidental "coincidences" happened. While searching through a box of clips for my Mother's Day column that's quoted in the previous chapter, I happened upon a column I'd written for that same North Carolina newspaper, this one dated December 10, 1989, under the headline "This snake's ruthless tale isn't funny anymore." My column opened with three rabbit punches intended to parody the Neuharth style: "I've worked for the S.O.B. I've read the S.O.B.'s book. And now, at long last, I've met the S.O.B." The column went on to describe a visit Neuharth paid to Greensboro to give a speech to business leaders and autograph copies of his just-published memoir. The column included this brief encounter:

> After Neuharth had finished autographing books at the Holiday Inn Four Seasons, I strolled with him to his waiting limousine. I noticed he was wearing a ring on his left hand that said "Founder USA TODAY" in diamonds about the size of raisins.
>
> "Is Bob Collins still with the company?" I asked.
>
> "Yes, he's the publisher of our paper in Camden, N.J.," Neuharth said.
>
> "He was a tough guy to work for."
>
> "Sure he was," Neuharth said with a smile.
>
> "It was like working in a salt mine."
>
> "Ha ha! I didn't know it was quite *that* bad. But Bob's a driver."
>
> "Yeah, he knocked me down to $140 a week."
>
> "Ha ha ha!" Neuharth said.
>
> "Is the company still hiring a lot of people right out of college?"
>
> "We hire some people out of college – but not for $140 a week."
>
> "Well, I guess that's progress."
>
> "Ha ha ha!" Neuharth said.
>
> As his gray limo eased into the driving sleet storm, it occurred to me that this self-proclaimed S.O.B. just might be the perfect emblem of the unscrupulous, acquisitive '80s.

I read these words in a state of amazement. I had no recollection of having read Neuharth's book when it first came out, or of interviewing him, or of writing that column. Zero. How could I erase such an elaborate chain of memories? Sure, I wrote the column a quarter of a century ago, and that's enough time to forget plenty of things, including the contents of a badly written book, a brief encounter with its reptilian author, and the ephemeral newspaper column that resulted. But this, I have to believe, is something more than mere forgetfulness with the passage of time. I must have willed myself to forget. Why?

I began to do the math. In December of 1989, Al Neuharth was sixty-five years old, freshly retired as head of the nation's biggest newspaper chain, a millionaire many times over who had just given a speech to the adoring business community, signed copies of his execrable book, then boarded a limo that carried him to the airport where his private jet awaited. The man had bled his employees dry so he could live like a maharaja. And because Americans worship the rich, especially the self-made rich, the business community had come out that day to fawn over Neuharth and make him a little bit richer. His book, of course, became a bestseller.

On that day I was a thirty-seven-year-old jackleg newspaper columnist who, a dozen years earlier, had gotten my start as a professional writer working in a salt mine run by the maharaja who'd just ridden off in the gray limo. In those dozen years I'd written four books and had nothing to show for it but a tall stack of rejection letters. Undaunted, I was working on a new book, a novel. I'm not ashamed to say that those unsold manuscripts aspired to the level of art, and sometimes attained it. And I'm not damning myself with faint praise when I say that the quality of the writing outshone anything to be found in *Confessions of an S.O.B.*

And now I began to understand the source of my willed forgetting of Neuharth's book, my brief encounter with the man, and the column. Was I exploited by him? Absolutely. Was I bitter? Absolutely not. The reason I wasn't bitter was because Al Neuharth, through his hired gun Bob Collins, gave me a chance to start working toward my dream of becoming a novelist. And in fairness, Neuharth had virtues much loftier than his knack for making money. He promoted the hiring of women and minorities in a business long dominated by white males. Indeed, roughly half of the employees in the *Public Opinion* newsroom, including the city editor, were women.

Maybe my forgetfulness came from the fact that I was ashamed that I shared Bob Collins's belief that being exploited by Gannett was part of a "fair tradeoff." Maybe I was afraid this branded me a hopeless chump. Or maybe what I really needed to forget was the lopsidedness of the circumstances of the media mogul inside the limo and the newspaper columnist standing outside in the sleet—that is, the gulf between the things that get revered and rewarded in America and the things that get ignored. That gulf, the immensity of it, was something I would have to accept—or forget or ignore—if I planned to continue pursuing my dream of becoming a serious writer as opposed to a rich hack. Americans, I was being reminded, have never had much use for serious writing. And so, without even realizing it, I forgot my encounter with Al Neuharth for a quarter of a century, until the discovery of an old column unlocked the buried memory. Forgetting, in this case, was a survival mechanism.

BY FAR THE MOST CHILLING passage in *Confessions of an S.O.B.* is the "report card" written by Loretta Helgeland, Neuharth's high school sweetheart who became his first wife. Their marriage lasted twenty-six years and produced a son and a daughter before ending in divorce in 1972, the year before Neuharth ascended the throne at Gannett. It was Loretta's snapshot of the life of the corporate wife that chilled me:

> In the final year of our marriage, (son) Dan was preparing to go away to college and (daughter) Jan was in her own world with high school friends. I won a Blue Ribbon in a flower

arranging show and was interviewed by a reporter. That night I read the newspaper column to the three of them: "Loretta Neuharth Loves Family, Gardening and Art." That headline summed it up. It made me feel so special, but Al, Dan and Jan paid me only ho-hum compliments on my award. The family cheerleader was finding it hard to get anyone to cheer her.

Loretta Neuharth's story about her Blue Ribbon for flower arranging made me think of Sue Collins. I thought of the pictures of Sue's Irish Setter show dogs, her Irish Setter wall clock, her Irish Setter statuette. "You really do go nuts with this," she had told me as she let the dogs out into the backyard. "I don't even try to explain it to myself. I just do it."

When she said that, I now realize, she was talking about much more than Irish Setters.

One-Way Ticket

A s the winter wore on, I kept sending out résumés, but no one was hiring. Or at least no one was hiring a reporter with barely a year's worth of experience writing about schools, colorful nobodies, and dark doings in a Pennsylvania backwater. There was nothing to do but keep sending out résumés, keep grinding, keep writing about the ninth guy on the bench.

My writing had come a long way, but I knew I was still far from being able to write publishable fiction. It might even be possible to illustrate how I knew this to be true. For a feature article on the graveyard shift at Chambersburg Hospital, I spent a long winter night hanging out with the hospital's little people—night nurses, security guards, X-ray techs, and a pregnant couple named Barry and Paula Trail who, when her water broke, had to ride a tractor and then a toboggan from their snowbound rural home to reach the ambulance waiting for them on the nearest paved road. It rushed them to the delivery room, where their healthy baby boy, six-pound, three-ounce Christopher, came into the world shortly before 3:00 a.m. Here's how I described the scene:

> The few corridor lights that are on give off brilliant white light. Here on the ground floor of the Chambersburg Hospital, the early morning is quiet and still.

Then the calm is punctured by the cries of a woman in labor. Her cries come down the corridor and through that doorway to Associate Director of Nursing Fay Gaugler and Virginia Gordon, the two nurses standing at the desk in the maternity ward. The quiet of the night seems to amplify the expectant mother's cries. She sounds very alone. But she is not.

With Paula Trail in these last painful moments before the birth of her first child is her husband Barry, their physician, Dr. Stuart Dittmar, and the delivery room staff.

And out by the desk the nurses and I are talking about the changing attitudes toward childbirth and about the growing trend of fathers participating in the process. I try to keep the conversation moving – to make Paula Trail's cries go away?

There's nothing wrong with this writing, certainly not for a small-town newspaper. But compare it with the fiction of a master, Denis Johnson, whose short story, "Car Crash While Hitchhiking," also winds up in a hospital. The narrator, the unnamed hitchhiker of the title, was asleep in the back seat of a couple's Oldsmobile when it was involved in a horrific crash. Later, at the hospital, the hitchhiker watches the wife enter. Notice how differently Johnson handles two of the details I'd noticed during my night at Chambersburg Hospital, namely the light in the hallway and the woman's scream:

Down the hall came the wife. She was glorious, burning. She didn't know yet that her husband was dead. We knew. That's what gave her such power over us. The doctor took her into a room with a desk at the end of the hall, and from under the door a slab of brilliance radiated as if, by some stupendous process, diamonds were being incinerated in there. What a pair of lungs! She shrieked as I imagined an eagle would shriek. It felt wonderful to be alive to hear it! I've gone looking for that feeling everywhere.

The wife was *glorious, burning.* A slab of light was so brilliant it might have come from some *stupendous* process, as though *diamonds were being incinerated.* The woman didn't just shriek, she shrieked as the narrator imagined an *eagle* would shriek. It felt *wonderful* (!) to be alive to hear it, and he has gone looking for that feeling everywhere.

What a glorious, unhinged bit of drama, all told in a few dozen words. No doubt about it, I still had a long way to go.

IN MARCH, AS MY SECOND Pennsylvania winter was getting tired of kicking me around, I got my first job nibble. One of the dozens of résumés I'd lobbed out into the world made its way indirectly to the editors of *The Greensboro Record,* the afternoon paper in the same North Carolina city where not so long ago I'd vacuumed the shag carpeting in the Record Bar. This, for once, was a genuine coincidence. At my father's urging I'd sent my résumé to the paper in Roanoke, Virginia, where a distant cousin of his was executive editor. He didn't offer me a job, but he passed my résumé and clips along to Greensboro, which was also part of the Norfolk, Virginia-based Landmark Communications chain, the company that would soon give the world the Weather Channel, which it would eventually sell for the handsome sum of $3.5 billion. The editors in Greensboro wanted me to come down for an interview, even offered to buy me a round-trip plane ticket and put me up in a hotel overnight. No more hitchhiking to job interviews. I had come up in the world.

This coincidence was more than a little unnerving. It was in Greensboro, at my sister Gretchen's college graduation in the spring of 1977, that I saw my mother for the last time. I still have a picture of her by the magnolia tree in my sister's front yard, hamming it up for the camera. She looked so full of life, so proud and happy. Two weeks later she was dead.

But I wasn't going to let that memory stop me from going back to Greensboro to see what there was to see. I was met at the airport by Ken Baldwin, head of the paper's human resources department, a dapper, little man with a whisk-broom moustache and dancing eyes. I remember feeling pleased that the paper had sent the head of the personnel department out to fetch me. As we drove in from the airport, I remarked on the dozens of loblolly pine trees bent to the ground and snapped like toothpicks. Had a tornado touched down? There had been an ice storm, Baldwin explained, and power had been knocked out for days in some areas. These storms, he added, were not uncommon in the spring-time. Despite the evidence of the recent storm, the sky was an implausibly soft blue—"Carolina blue," as it was known locally—and the day felt nearly balmy compared to what I'd left behind that morning in Pennsylvania. Something inside me began to thaw.

By the end of the day I'd talked to so many editors I was punch drunk. Late in the proceedings, one of them actually asked me what I saw myself doing five years from now, and I had to restrain myself from climbing over the desk and going for his throat. But I kept myself in check, and by the end of the long day they offered me a job covering the University of North Carolina's board of governors, the state Board of Education, the local public schools, and the five colleges in town. Like Bob Collins, they promised me I would have plenty of time to pursue my own "enterprise" stories. Then came the clincher: they were willing to nearly double my pay. It wasn't *The Washington Post*'s "Style" section, and I didn't want to spend the rest of my life covering school-board meetings—who in their right mind would?—but it was a one-way ticket out of Chambersburg, and, I told myself, the winters were mild in Piedmont, North Carolina, and the place was nestled midway between the Blue Ridge Mountains and the Outer Banks. Playing coy, I told the editors I would need a little time to think it over.

That night I wanted to decompress and celebrate, so I walked to a popular restaurant called Ham's, not far from the house where I'd once slept on my sister's sofa. Walking into Ham's that night was like walking into a madhouse. The NCAA men's basketball tournament was on television, and in a fearful bit of symmetry, Duke, located an hour east of Greensboro in Durham, was playing the University of Pennsylvania. This mob was solidly behind Duke, which, I was informed, had just won the Atlantic Coast Conference tournament at the Greensboro Coliseum. Of course I had heard about college basketball mania in North Carolina, but this was the first time I'd been physically swept up into it. Each Duke basket was greeted with roared cheers and spilled beers. The place and everyone in it was sticky. These people were glorious, burning. After two frigid winters in a Pennsylvania monastery, it felt wonderful to be in such a place.

When I got back to Chambersburg, Maude and I talked things over, and even though you're never supposed to take the first job offer you get, we agreed I should take this one. I would go down to Greensboro alone and see what the job and the town were like. If things looked promising, Maude would quit her job at the Waynesboro paper and come down and join me.

The next day I went to tell Collins, but his office was dark and empty. His secretary stunned me with the news that he no longer worked there. I went back to the newsroom, where Katy Hamilton told me Collins had gone through the drill he would describe to me five years later on the deserted streets of Shadow

Lake. Word had come down from Rochester yesterday, Katy explained, then a car arrived at Collins's house and drove him to the airport in Hagerstown, where the corporate jet was waiting. It flew him to Pittsburgh, and the next day—today—he took over as president and publisher of Gannett's *Valley News Dispatch*, the paper where Brad Bumsted was working.

I didn't even get a chance to say thank you or good-bye to the man who'd given me my first break.

A FEW HOURS AFTER I reported for work in Greensboro, a smiling Ken Baldwin walked up to my desk and said, "Professor Gleason says hello."

I had taken Tom Gleason's Russian History course in college, and like a lot of his students, I gravitated to his book-lined office for lively discussions that roamed far afield from the Decembrists and the Bolsheviks. Gleason freely loaned books from his shelves—but only after the borrower signed a ledger and vowed to return the volume. When I decided I wanted to undertake an independent-study project on the history of Providence, Gleason and another history professor, Howard Chudacoff, encouraged me and agreed to be my faculty sponsors.

Now Ken Baldwin lingered at my desk, obviously delighted by the surprise on my face. I had given Tom Gleason as a reference on my résumé, never dreaming that employers actually checked with references. Baldwin said, "He spoke very highly of you—except for one thing."

"What's that?" I asked, flummoxed.

"He says you borrowed a book about the October Uprising from him and never returned it."

I realized it was true. I'd thought the statute of limitations had run out, but I was busted.

Baldwin laughed. "Welcome aboard."

THAT EXCHANGE WITH KEN BALDWIN came back to me three years later when I heard the news that *The Washington Post* was returning a Pulitzer Prize, because it had come out that the prize-winning reporter, Janet Cooke, had fabricated her story about an eight-year-old DC heroin addict known only by his alias, "Jimmy." I had read Cooke's story when it was published in September of 1980 and, like millions of others, I had the *holy shit!* reaction Ben Bradlee said he was always trying to elicit from *Post* readers.

What intrigued me about the "Jimmy" fiasco was not the fact that a reporter had fabricated a story, but that a reporter had virtually fabricated herself, and no one at the paper that toppled Nixon had bothered to cross-check either fiction. According to her résumé, Janet Cooke had graduated from Vassar. The biographical information she submitted to the Pulitzer judges made the additional claims that she had studied at the Sorbonne and was proficient in French, Spanish, Portuguese, and Italian. None of it was true. What was true was that Janet Cooke was a black woman who, when she wasn't writing fiction, had undeniable talent and potential as a journalist.

"Her Vassar credentials were never checked," Bradlee would write in his memoir. "This was our first mistake, and it was fatal . . . How come we never checked? Simply put, because Janet Cooke was too good to be true, and we wanted her too bad. . . . At a time when we were struggling to meet our commitment to increase the quantity and quality of minority and female journalists on the paper, Janet Cooke had 'can't miss' written all over her. What the hell were we waiting for? Grab her before *The New York Times* does, or *Newsweek*, or television. And she was hired."

These missteps fascinated me not because of something as tawdry as *schadenfreude*, the joy people derive from the distress of others, literally "damage joy" in German. I had no hard feelings toward Ben Bradlee or *The Washington Post*. No, what fascinated me was the way the Janet Cooke story illustrated the fact that there's a right way and a wrong way to do certain things, and an institution's or an individual's fame or wealth or power doesn't buy them an exemption from that fact. In the not insignificant matter of checking the accuracy of a job applicant's credentials, the middling *Greensboro Record* had outperformed the mighty *Washington Post*. This minor mistake on the *Post*'s part opened the door to the monster mistake: editors, including Bradlee, being so gulled by a reporter's fictionalized self that they were willing to buy her fictionalized reporting without even the most rudimentary fact-checking.

Actually, that's not quite fair. There were skeptics on the *Post* staff, editors and reporters who were uneasy about Janet Cooke's persona and her reporting. It could be the tiniest detail that rang false, but the tiny detail, as all writers know, is where God and the devil dwell. David Maraniss, a *Post* reporter and editor who would go on to win a Pulitzer Prize he actually got to keep, distrusted Cooke's claim that "Jimmy" was a Baltimore Orioles fan. "No fucking way, inner-city kid in Washington would be an Orioles fan," Maraniss would say later. "Baseball even. Maybe a Redskins fan or a Bullets fan, not an Orioles fan. So I just thought that was so wrong . . ."

Reporter Mike Sager thought the black dialog in Cooke's story "sounded like a white person imitating jive." Vivian Aplin-Brownlee, Cooke's immediate editor, claimed she never believed the "Jimmy" story. Courtland Milloy, a black Metro reporter, became skeptical when he drove Cooke around DC's tough Condon Terrace neighborhood, and Cooke couldn't find the house where "Jimmy" supposedly lived. Despite these misgivings, the story ran on the front page with the enthusiastic endorsement of both Bradlee and Bob Woodward, then an assistant managing editor and no stranger to the delicate dance of protecting confidential sources. When the story was nominated for the Pulitzer, the chorus of doubters grew louder. But without proof it was impossible to stop the train as it hurtled toward disaster.

AS I PLUNGED INTO my new job, memories of Chambersburg began a surprisingly quick fade. Even the most vivid moments—interviewing Merle Unger's mother in the courthouse hallway, interviewing Scott Reichenbach in his hospital bed, losing Amos, burying my mother, enduring Ben Bradlee's salty monolog, getting praised or blistered by Bob Collins—it all turned to smoke. I suppose this is because a reporter for a daily newspaper is always looking forward, never back, always chasing today's story and never lingering over what happened yesterday. History is for historians.

But memories, as we have seen, rarely die completely. They may lie dim and dormant for years and then, thanks to some spark, come jittering back to imperfect life. That certainly happened the day I walked into the New York art gallery and discovered the photographs of Arnold Odermatt and *bango!* flashed back to all those pictures of car wrecks in *Public Opinion* thirty years earlier. Those memories jump-started something that had been sleeping inside me. They made me realize I had witnessed and written about some remarkable things long ago in a small Pennsylvania town, things that might be revisited and revived and made into a book.

So after seeing Odermatt's pictures, I went online and looked up Katy Hamilton in Chambersburg, Pennsylvania. There she was, still listed at 343 Lincoln Way West, which, if memory served, was where she lived when I worked at *Public Opinion.* I could see it again—a rickety frame apartment building just up the hill to the west of the town square. I dialed the number and held my breath. Either I was meant to write a book or I was not, and I would know the answer in a few seconds. The phone rang half a dozen times, eight, ten. Just as I was about to give up, someone picked up the phone. The first thing I heard was the tones of an emergency code, then a dispatcher's voice directing emergency crews to the scene of some calamity. Finally, in her unmistakable German accent, Katy said, "Hallo?" I was on my way.

We reminisced for a long time as her police scanner crackled in the background. Though she had retired from the paper a dozen years earlier, Katy said she was still addicted to this lo-fi river of information about the dramas, large and small, that make up day-to-day life in Chambersburg and every other town in the world, the fender benders and fatal wrecks, the shoplifting and the shootings, the domestic disputes and barroom brawls, the fires and missing persons and lost dogs. "After all these years," Katy said, "I couldn't live without it."

As I tracked down more of my former colleagues, I discovered that most of us shared surprisingly warm feelings about our time at *Public Opinion*. There was an *esprit de corps* in that newsroom, we agreed, and we were all brimming with idealism and energy and faith in the power of the press to make the world a better place. We were young, and we were so in love with the work we were doing that we were willing to forget that we were being shamelessly exploited by a rapacious corporation.

When David Scott Smith and I got to reminiscing, he said something about our lives in Chambersburg that neither of us quite expected. "I got no complaints about it," he said. "It was a great place to start out." Then, after a pause, he sounded surprised to hear himself add, "I kinda miss it."

So do I, I realized. And that was when I knew that "it" was a book.

Acknowledgments

This book exists because countless people were willing to share their stories, insights, photographs, files, and memories with me. Chief among them are my former colleagues at *Public Opinion*, including Brad Bumsted, Dawn DeCwikiel-Kane, Katy Hamilton, Marie Lanser, and David Scott Smith.

I learned about the back alleys of Chambersburg, the zeitgeist of the '70s, the minds of murderers, the artistry of John Waters, and hundreds of other things from a loose posse of friends, relatives, and talkative strangers, including Dan Epstein, Ken Gibble, David Kane, my sister Gretchen Kelly, my late father Richard Morris, Dick North, Ken Peiffer, Maude Scott, Bob Vucic, and Ted and Karen Wingerd.

My research was enriched by the current staff at *Public Opinion*, by Ruth Gembe and the rest of the staff at the Coyle Free Library in Chambersburg, and by the staffs at the Alexander Hamilton Memorial Free Library in Waynesboro, Pennsylvania, and the Washington County Library in Hagerstown, Maryland.

This book benefited immensely from the invisible and highly talented hand of its editor, Janice Rhayem, and from the rest of the crew at Sunbury Press, especially Lawrence Knorr and Crystal Devine. As always,

I'm indebted to my agent, Alice Martell, a writer's dream advocate.

Finally, special thanks to three selfless and courageous firefighters—Bill Kady, Bob Monn and, above all, Scott Reichenbach, who gave me a gift that changed my life forever, and changed it for the better. And eternal thanks to Marianne, light of my life.

Sources

To research this book, I read hundreds of back issues of *Public Opinion*, the Waynesboro (PA) *Record Herald*, and the Hagerstown (MD) *Morning Herald*. For the early history of central Pennsylvania, I turned to *The History of Franklin County, Pa.* by Samuel P. Bates. For Chambersburg's role in the Civil War, I relied on *Battle Cry of Freedom* by James McPherson and "The Burning of Chambersburg" by Liva Baker in *American Heritage* magazine. John Brown's visits to Chambersburg on the eve of the assault on Harpers Ferry were brought to vivid life by two books: *John Brown in Chambersburg* by Virginia Ott Stake; and the terrific novel *The Good Lord Bird* by James McBride, winner of the National Book Award.

The story of the Shade Gap crime spree comes from news accounts, the book *Deadly Pursuit* by Robert V. Cox, and author interviews with Ken Peiffer. For background on Mennonite beliefs and practices, I drew on *Pennsylvania: Seed of a Nation* by Paul A.W. Wallace. The story of Debbie Sue Kline's kidnapping and murder comes from news accounts and the books *Missing Person* by Cox and Peiffer, and *Dorothy Allison: A Psychic Story* by Dorothy Allison and Scott Jacobson, as well as author interviews with Peiffer and Marie Lanser.

The section on Gary Lee Rock's crimes comes from trial transcripts, news accounts, personal memories, the book *The Last Alarm* by Jerry Laughlin, and author interviews with Dawn DeCwikiel-Kane, Ken Gibble, Bill Kady, Bob Monn, Ken Peiffer, Scott Reichenbach, and David Scott Smith.

For the story about my job interview at *The Washington Post* and the Janet Cooke fiasco, I relied on personal memories, the memories and old clips of my father, and the books *A Good Life* by Benjamin C. Bradlee and *Yours in Truth: A Personal Portrait of Ben Bradlee* by Jeff Himmelman.

Other books that informed my writing include: *Speedboat* by Renata Adler; *Libra* by Don DeLillo; *Slouching Towards Bethlehem* by Joan Didion; *Forgetting: Myths, Perils and Compensations* by Douwe Draaisma; *Otherwise Known as the Human Condition* by Geoff Dyer; *Southerners* by Marshall Frady; *City on Fire* by Garth Risk Hallberg; *The Journalist and the Murderer* by Janet Malcolm; *Confessions of an S.O.B.* by Al Neuharth; *The Moviegoer* by Walker Percy; and *American Pastoral* by Philip Roth.

Author Bio

Since leaving Chambersburg and *Public Opinion*, Bill Morris has published three critically acclaimed novels—*Motor City, All Souls' Day*, and *Motor City Burning*—and has written for numerous daily newspapers, websites and magazines, including *The New York Times, Granta, The Washington Post Magazine, L.A. Weekly, The* (London) *Independent, The Greensboro* (NC) *News & Record, Popular Mechanics*, and *The Daily Beast*. He currently lives in New York City, where he's a staff writer with the online literary magazine *The Millions*.

CPSIA information can be obtained
at www.ICGtesting.com
Printed in the USA
LVOW08s1723130317
527031LV00002B/444/P